HOPKINS'S POETICS OF SPEECH SOUND:
SPRUNG RHYTHM, LETTERING, INSCAPE

from the keep, Carisbrooke
Castle.
July 25.

G.M. Hopkins, 'From the Keep. Carisbrooke Castle [Isle of Wight]. July 25 [1863].' The drawing evokes Hopkins's lifelong Ruskin-inspired interest in medieval architecture (see 'Conclusion'). By permission, University of Texas, Harry Ransom Humanities Research Center.

JAMES I. WIMSATT

Hopkins's Poetics of Speech Sound

Sprung Rhythm, Lettering, Inscape

UNIVERSITY OF TORONTO PRESS
Toronto Buffalo London

© University of Toronto Press Incorporated 2006
Toronto Buffalo London
Printed in Canada

ISBN-13: 978-0-8020-9154-3
ISBN-10: 0-8020-9154-7

Printed on acid-free paper

Library and Archives Canada Cataloguing in Publication

Wimsatt, James I.
    Hopkins' poetics of speech sound : sprung rhythm,
lettering, inscape / James I. Wimsatt.

    Includes bibliography and index.
    ISBN 0-8020-9154-7

    1. Hopkins, Gerard Manley, 1844–1889 – Versification.
    2. Poetics.   I. Title.

PR4803.H44Z97 2006   821.8   C2006-903340-4

University of Toronto Press acknowledges the financial assistance to
its publishing program of the Canada Council for the Arts and the
Ontario Arts Council.

Contents

Acknowledgments

To begin at the beginning, I must acknowledge my debt to Hopkins scholarship, an important part of which is represented in the bibliography. The editorial tradition of the poetry, from Robert Bridges until today, which has culminated in Norman H. MacKenzie's excellent *Poetical Works* and facsimiles of the manuscripts, is a tribute not only to the editor, but to modern editorial practice and to Oxford University Press. I might add that, now that students have the Catherine Phillips edition of *The Major Works*, Hopkins scholars would be further well served by the Press's bringing back into print MacKenzie's edition of the poetry with its full textual and explanatory notes, cited here by permission, and by a new, more complete collection, or at least a reprint, of the *Journals and Papers*.

The Hopkins critical tradition is ample and strong. From my observation, its main lack is a greater scholarly consciousness of the full range and value of the poet's prose writings. But this is to find fault amid plenty. As my text and bibliography indicate, I have found much useful information and astute analysis in a wide range of sources. To the many authors and presses that have made Hopkins's poetry and his thought so accessible to common understanding and application I am unreservedly thankful. Essential to me, of course, has been the generous help from individuals and institutions that I have received at all stages in the book's development. The work has been so long in the making, and so many scholars and friends have contributed important insights, that I am afraid that I will be unable to remember and acknowledge all of their good advice. The following is what I recall at this time. For all assistance, both named and unnamed, I am indeed grateful.

Among the individuals to whom I am indebted for their counsel and suggestions, certain ones are especially notable: Tom Cable, who has been with me all the way, willingly reading and discreetly commenting on and questioning prosodic matters in the manuscript; John Sheriff, who shared with me his formidable knowledge of Charles Sanders Peirce and led me on a pleasant visit to the Peirce home at Milford, Pennsylvania; Terry Kelley for her very helpful critique; Jorie Woods and Tony Glover for their useful leads on the rhetoric tradition; Scott Miers for his phonological understanding; variously, Terry Brogan, Jay Hill, Bill Kibler, Fred Chappell, Tom Kirby-Smith, Ted Wright, and Jerry Bump; Larry Earp for his musical expertise; and Michael Suarez, S.J., who welcomed me at Campion College, Oxford, and made the major Hopkins archive there available. I owe special thanks to Louis Mackey, recently deceased, who not only gave me important insight into the vexed matter of inscape, but throughout my time at the University of Texas offered a consummate model of erudite philosopher, indefatigable teacher, and informed literary analyst.

The libraries and librarians at the University of Texas at Austin and the University of Scranton have been of major assistance. I am conscious also of the substantial gratitude I owe to the editors and the anonymous readers of journal essays that I have published along the way in *Modern Language Quarterly*, *Style*, *Speculum*, and especially to Meir Sternberg, editor of *Poetics Today*, and to that journal's readers of my essay on Hopkins's rhymes, which I use extensively in chapter 3 by permission. I am very fortunate in that all of the journal editors and readers were uniformly rigorous and fair in their evaluations and suggestions and often led me to new understandings.

A fortiori, I am grateful to Jill McConkey, editor at the University of Toronto Press, to all the Press's editorial staff, and to the very knowledgeable and demanding readers who saw the manuscript through a major recasting. The revised ordering in the presentation of the book's argument and the introduction of new materials that they led me to particularly strengthened the work.

Finally, I will not try to express the many ways that my wife, Rebecca Beal, exemplary teacher, scholar, computer nerd extraordinaire, and mother, made this book possible; or my debt to our fourteen-year-old son, David, who has kept me moving despite my desire to just chill out. My other children, Andrew and Alison, years older, have provided less insistent inspirational encouragement. I dedicate *Hopkins's Poetics of Speech Sound* to Rebecca.

The book is published with the generous support of a University Cooperative Society Subvention Grant awarded by the University of Texas at Austin. The Co-op has long been a favourite resource for me, and once again I have good reason to be thankful for its assistance.

Abbreviations

The following abbreviations for Hopkins's works are used throughout the text. Full publication details are provided in the Works Cited.

J   *The Journals and Papers of Gerard Manley Hopkins*
LI   *The Letters of Gerard Manley Hopkins to Robert Bridges*
LII   *The Correspondence of Gerard Manley Hopkins and Richard Watson Dixon*
LIII *Further Letters of Gerard Manley Hopkins*
LIV *Selected Letters*
MSII *The Later Poetic Manuscripts of Gerard Manley Hopkins*
P   *The Poetical Works of Gerard Manley Hopkins*

Note: Unless otherwise indicated, all emphases in extracts are original.

HOPKINS'S POETICS OF SPEECH SOUND:
SPRUNG RHYTHM, LETTERING, INSCAPE

Introduction:
Hopkins's Manifesto – 'Poetry and Verse'

This book is about Gerard Manley Hopkins's theory of poetry as expressed in his prose writings, not in the first place about his verse. Numerous fine interpretive studies and books have been written on the poetry, but since I deal here with his poetic theory, there are limited occasions on which to cite such criticism. At the same time, because his poetry often provides some of the best support for his theoretical statements, I do instance Hopkins's poetic practice repeatedly. In combining to form a coherent and impressive poetics of speech sound, Hopkins's theoretical writings, which lie fragmentary and scattered among his diaries, student essays, correspondence, and poetic manuscripts, centre on phonetic aspects, even as the phonic patterns of his verse constitute the most distinctive feature of his poetry.

To say that the sounds are the most characteristic and also the most prominent feature of the poetry is not to deny the force of his vivid verbal representations. It is rather to emphasize that an overriding aspect of his verse is the impressively complex matrix of sound formed by the rhythms, the phonetic designs of the lines, feet, and stanzas, and the end-rhymes, alliterations, and vowel gradations. Similarly, Hopkins's most significant statement on the nature of poetry, the brief and incomplete essay entitled 'Poetry and Verse,' is almost entirely devoted to features of speech sound. It was probably written in 1873–4, a year or two before the foundering of the *Deutschland* provided the occasion of Hopkins's first work in sprung rhythm. In manuscript, 'Poetry and Verse' is appended to a much longer text, 'Rhythm and Other Structural Parts of Rhetoric – Verse,' also dealing mainly with aspects of verse sound. The longer work seems to comprise notes for a lecture, as his editors indicate, but the appended 'Poetry and Verse' is too speculative in nature to have served for the usual lecturing purposes, as they further conjecture (J xxvii). Because of its parentheses and constricted explanations it is a vexing piece, yet it contains a body of succinct theoretical statements that assert a coherent groundbreaking concept of the poetical – of poeticalness – as embodied in speech sound. It provides a strong basis on which to rest his explanation of poeticalness: that which distinguishes the poetical in discourse.

Insofar as 'manifesto' implies a public proclamation of an intellectual program, to label 'Poetry and Verse' a 'manifesto' is a gross overstatement; not only is it incomplete, but also it had no early audience and Hopkins did not seek one for it. Insofar as the word indicates – manifests – a firm and lasting declaration of principles, however, it is valid. The essay answers in a new and productive way the old question of what constitutes poetry. Hopkins begins by stating, tamely enough, that just as all versified language is not poetry, neither is all poetry verse. But then he becomes less anodyne, declaring that poetry is a particular form of speech, not at all meaning that it is a form of rhetoric; rather, he is presenting the poetical as constituted by speech sound. He begins by asking, 'Is all verse poetry or all poetry verse?' and responds permissively that it 'Depends on definitions of both.' His own answer that follows belies the permissiveness:

> Poetry is speech framed for contemplation of the mind by the way of hearing or speech framed to be heard for its own sake and interest even over and above its interest of meaning.

That the words should make substantial sense is requisite, he continues, but the subject and the verbal significance are subordinate to the 'shape,' the phonetic design, which carries the 'inscape' of speech:

> Some matter and meaning is essential to it but only as an element necessary to support and employ the shape which is contemplated for its own sake. (Poetry is in fact speech only employed to carry the inscape of speech for the inscape's sake – and therefore the inscape must be dwelt on.)

'Inscape' is a coinage of Hopkins and the key term in his metaphysics and poetics. The word is modelled on terms, such as 'landscape' or 'seascape,' that refer to visual scenes and, of course, it suggests something like 'inner landscape.' He explains it to Robert Bridges as 'design, pattern' (LI 66); showing that he means more than superficial pattern, he identifies it to Richard Dixon as 'the very soul of art' (LII 135). He developed the term while he was still at Oxford, and it became central to his writings, even as the concept became central in his thought. Beyond the obvious implications of the word there is only a vague critical consensus on inscape's meaning, and it is still not common in dictionaries. The poet's usages leave plenty of room for puzzlement, but that does not indicate confusion on his part, as I will try to show when I undertake full discussion of its implications in chapter 4.

In 'Poetry and Verse,' following a statement that what is necessary for poetry is that it should reveal the inscape of the particular speech, he asserts unequivocally that neither the lexical substance nor the repetitions of verse form are of the essence:

> Now if this [revelation of the inscape] can be done without repeating it[,] *once* of the inscape will be enough for art and beauty and poetry but then at least the inscape must be understood as so standing by itself that it could be copied and repeated. If not/ repetition, *oftening, over-and-overing, aftering* of the inscape must take place in order to detach it to the mind and in this light poetry is speech which afters and oftens its inscape, speech couched in a repeating figure and verse is spoken sound having a repeating figure. Verse is (inscape of spoken sound, not spoken words, or speech employed to carry the inscape of spoken sound – or in the usual words) speech wholly or partially repeating the same figure of sound.

The repetitions that aid detachment of speech inscape, the poet goes on to assert, are not themselves necessarily of verse form; the repetitions may be figures of grammar. One supposes that here he is making a place in his definition for the incantatory repetitions found in the Bible, or the work of poets such as Christopher Smart, William Blake, or Walt Whitman, as well as repetitions used in well-formed prose:

> Now there is speech which wholly or partially repeats the same figure of grammar and this may be framed to be heard for its own sake and interest over and above its interest of meaning. Poetry then may be couched in this, and therefore all poetry is not verse but all poetry is either verse or falls under this or some still further development of what verse is, speech wholly or partially repeating some kind of figure which is over and above meaning, at least the grammatical, historical, and logical meaning. (J 289)

Poetry requires making speech inscape available for contemplation. Verse serves as the usual way, but not the only way, for the poet to repeat 'figures of speech sound.'

Except for the examination of it by J. Hillis Miller (1966), 'Poetry and Verse' is a neglected text. Major treatments of Hopkins's poetics, such as Maria Lichtman's *Contemplative Poetry of Gerard Manley Hopkins* (1989) and Michael Sprinker's *A Counterpoint of Dissonance* (1980), have ignored it. Lichtman treats the poet's student essays as his significant theoretical statements, and Sprinker gives but short shrift to most of his prose statements in favour of treating his 'true kinship in ... the work of the French Symbolists' (31). Sprinker's attempt to show Hopkins as a 'sort of "Victorian Mallarmé"' takes his verse too far out of context. Lichtman's discussion of his poetry places it admirably in the frame of his theoretical statements, but she, like Roman Jakobson, relies largely on the early Platonic dialogue 'On the Origin of Beauty' (1865; J 86–114) in finding parallelism to be the key to his theory of poetry. In that essay, Hopkins treats 'poetry' and 'verse' as virtually synonymous. By contrast, in the later 'Poetry and Verse' (1873–4), his concern is to distinguish the two. In the eight years between composition of the essays, Hopkins developed his concept of inscape. Lichtman sees *parallelism* as both the forerunner and the meaning of both instress and inscape (7–33), but 'Poetry and Verse' makes clear that while the parallelisms of verse can be important in detaching inscape for the 'contemplation of the mind,' the quality of poeticalness is found in the 'inscape of speech' itself. Parallelism might be said to mark the exterior 'scape' of poetry, but it is not the interior 'inscape' of poetry: 'Poetry is in fact speech only employed to carry the inscape of speech for the inscape's sake.'

Hillis Miller makes much the same mistake in his discussions of Hopkins's idea of poetry. I will discuss his detailed examination of 'Poetry and Verse' in chapter 4. Nevertheless, it is apposite to quote at this point a summary statement in which he identifies inscape as 'rhyme,' much as Lichtman sees it as parallelism: 'Hopkins' theory of poetry as the inscape of speech for the inscape's sake has organized and conquered the whole realm of words through an extension of the principle of rhyme. Different modes of echoing mean that all words together form an elaborate system of interrelated reverberations. But in defining poetry in this way Hopkins has cut it off from the poet and from nature.' (1966, 96). Miller presents Hopkins as another whose poetry and theory have caught him in the prison-house of language. But 'Poetry and Verse' makes clear that the poet sees the 'reverberations' of language – the sound repetitions, parallelism and rhyme – as an instrument for *detaching* inscape, not the inscape itself, which is of the essence.

Hopkins's experience of teaching rhetoric at Roehampton early in his priesthood evidently prompted him to formulate his concept of poetry in 'Poetry and Verse.' When he wrote the text, he was twenty-nine and would live for sixteen years longer; in that time he composed the body of his major work. Virtually all of what he says in his critical writings subsequently is consistent with 'Poetry and Verse,' but he enriches and fills out the substance of its brief statement with other declarations in his diaries, correspondence, essays, and notes.

One major tenet of Hopkins's poetics, the essential place of rhythm as the fundamental organizing principle of speech sound, shows up especially in his later writings. It is consistent with the earlier piece in that for him either the regular rhythm of verse or the irregular rhythm of prose can make poetry. This insight makes clear the triumph that the poet saw in his innovative sprung rhythm: its reconciliation of the repetitions of verse rhythm, that help to reveal inscape, with the irregularities of prose rhythm that are typical of speech. He first used sprung rhythm in his long ode, *The Wreck of the Deutschland*, and he explained it in his important accompanying prefaces. He thought that his theoretical formulation was original, but he far from saw his own verse as the only representative of sprung rhythm. Variously, he cites as precedents *Piers Plowman*, Robert Greene, certain nursery rhymes, *Samson Agonistes*, and others. Nor did he think that the rhythm was the only adequate sound pattern for poetry: 'Rhythm in general' was poetry's concern. In his last years he was working enthusiastically on a book about Dorian measure (the measure of Pindar and other Greek lyricists) that might well have become his comprehensive art of rhythmic sound. The book was 'nominally' to concern the Dorian measure, he said, 'but with an introduction in the philosophy (for the speculation goes pretty deep) of rhythm in general' (LIII 277 [1887]). Whatever he wrote of the book seems lost, but 'Poetry and Verse' and especially his later correspondence indicate the direction of his thinking on this 'deep' problem.

Hopkins's characterizations of the poetical, both of speech sound as the substance of the poetical and of the nature of poetic rhythm, are indeed original, but they did not, of course, spring from his brain without parentage. In the first place, he read widely in classical Greek and Latin poetry and philosophy and in vernacular literature of all periods, especially English, and he developed opinions about most of his reading. The consequent influences on his poetics are manifold, a large

number of which Hopkins scholars have pointed out. Often they have
overemphasized particular vernacular traditions, claiming primacy of
influence on his poetry and verse practice for Old English, Celtic, or
Scandinavian verse. But they have neglected the underlying permeation
of both his thought and practice with classical poetry and rhetoric. At
Oxford his studies revolved largely around early Greek philosophy and
poetry; as a Jesuit he became teacher of rhetoric at Stonyhurst College in
Lancashire and later professor of Greek and fellow in classics in Dublin.
In his practice as scholar and poet the mark of the classics is everywhere,
extending to composition of poetry in both Latin and Greek. The
significance he attaches to speech sound notably accords with the ideas
of classical rhetoricians as they developed from the sophists to Isocrates
and Cicero. These rhetoricians saw in the patterns of speech sound what
Steven Katz calls an 'epistemic music,' a verbal music that carries affective or sensory meaning that is constitutive, a kind of meaning that
enters before the verbal sense is realized. Hopkins's concept of speech
inscape deepens this power, transferring it from the realm of rhetoric to
that of poetry – realms he clearly saw as separate, though coordinate. His
ideas about rhythm were based largely on Greek lyric practice, as his
description of his projected masterwork on 'rhythm in general' shows.

His friends, whose training generally was comparable to his in classical
language and literature, provided him with an important opportunity,
which he otherwise lacked after he joined the Jesuits, to develop and
enunciate his ideas. The correspondence with them, along with the
discussions of sprung rhythm prefaced to *Deutschland* and his annotations of his poetic texts, supply a continuation of the early papers in
elucidating the mature development of his poetics. Especially important
are his exchanges with his poet-friends, Robert Bridges, Canon Richard
Watson Dixon, and Coventry Patmore (collected, respectively, in LI, LII,
and LIII). The three shared with him broad assumptions about poetry.
Their concerns in large part were with prosodic matters, markedly those
characteristic of the later nineteenth century.

Of particular significance is Hopkins's correspondence with Bridges
that began shortly after their time together at Oxford. Bridges subsequently became Hopkins's dearest friend and certainly his most ardent
correspondent about verse. It is a poignant comment on the poets' close
relationship that Hopkins's last poem, the sonnet *To R.B.*, formed part
of his final letter to Bridges. The prime authority for both poets was
Milton. Bridges readily acknowledged that their exchanges about the
great poet's work and about poetry in general stimulated the early

development of his *Milton's Prosody*, still standard, whose prime concern, of course, is with poetic sound patterns. Though Bridges outlived Hopkins by over forty years and enjoyed long celebrity as poet laureate, he always kept his friend in his thoughts. Long after Hopkins's death he was corresponding regularly with the poet's mother, and at length in 1918 he brought to publication the bulk of the poetry that he had assiduously preserved.

While the letters that Bridges wrote to Hopkins unfortunately are not extant, both sides of Hopkins's correspondence with Canon Richard Watson Dixon (1833–1900) survive, including forty-one letters that Hopkins wrote between 1878 and 1888 (LII). Dixon briefly had been his teacher at Highgate School in the late 1850s; some fifteen years afterward, with apparently no contact in the time between, Hopkins sent the canon a letter praising his poetry and lamenting its general failure of recognition. Dixon replied gratefully, with obvious emotion, and a warm exchange of letters ensued that lasted till Hopkins's death. We also have twenty-six of Hopkins's letters to the still more senior, well-established poet, Coventry Patmore (1823–96), together with Patmore's replies (LIII). The two met in 1883 on the older poet's visit to Stonyhurst College when Hopkins was teaching there. Like Bridges, Patmore published important works on verse theory, and certain aspects of Hopkins's ideas, especially those on verse timing, seem influenced by his *Prefatory Study of English Metrical Law* (cf. Holloway, 82–100), though Patmore evidently was baffled by Hopkins's fresh concepts.

The correspondence between Hopkins and Bridges, Dixon, and Patmore was stimulated especially by a common overriding interest in verse technique. The personal relationships between the poets that the letters evidence are telling. With Bridges Hopkins was sometimes deferential and enquiring. 'I shd. be glad,' Hopkins asks, for example, 'if you wd. explain what a [sonnet] *coda* is and how employed' (LI 246); yet in his commentary on poetics and his analysis of Bridges's verse he would more often instruct and admonish than query and praise: 'The verse paragraphs drag; they are not perfectly achieved' (LI 68) is a typical comment. At one point, the severity of his remarks even led Bridges to doubt his own abilities. Hopkins, being entirely confident of his own idiosyncratic opinions but not essentially rigid, seems surprised at Bridges's insecurity: 'You ask whether I really think there is any good in your going on writing poetry' (LI 93) he notes and proceeds to reassure him of his high esteem and the worth of his verse. On the other side, while Bridges obviously took to heart Hopkins's negative comments, he was not bashful about returning the favour. He made clear that he was put off by the difficulties of the *Deutschland* ode and by sprung rhythm; but his criticism hardly fazed Hopkins, who ultimately to some degree converted Bridges to the rhythm. Predictably, the stickler Hopkins found his friend's mastery of the method incomplete: 'The pieces in sprung rhythm – do not quite satisfy me' (LI 71); and, commenting to Dixon, 'Bridges treats [sprung rhythm] in theory and practice as something informal and variable without any limit but ear and taste, but this is not how I look at it' (LII 39).

In contrast to Bridges, who generally discussed poetic matters with Hopkins as an equal, Hopkins's two other poet-correspondents, Dixon and Patmore, were rather awed by his learning, analytic powers, and infinite attention to matters of form and phonetics. While Patmore, when dealing with others, habitually assumed an authoritative stance on poetics, he is quite deferential to Father Hopkins: 'Your careful and subtle fault-finding is the greatest tribute my poetry has ever received' (LIII 324–5). Dixon is even more respectful, 'I wish I could express how much I think of you, & feel with you, & how grateful I am for your criticism & opinion' (LII 71). This is not to say that they readily accepted Hopkins's sprung rhythm and his more opaque poetry, but they characteristically attributed their difficulties to their own inadequacies. As a result, Hopkins's letters to them are valuable particularly for his elaborations of matters such as classical metrics and sprung rhythm. Hopkins's eagerness to convert Bridges to his ideas sometimes led him beyond his usual exposition and critique: 'You say you wd. not for any money read my poem [the *Deutschland*]. Nevertheless I beg you will. Besides money, you know, there is love' (LI 146). Their very directness with each other, of course, testifies to the love between them.

Aspects of Hopkins's poetics show up in specific commentary on his own and his correspondents' verse and in his more general observations to them about rhythm, accent, quantity, form, and, most important, in his extensive discussions of sprung rhythm. Thus, while his basic explanations of sprung rhythm are in the 'Preface' and 'Note on Sprung Rhythm,' which accompany the manuscript texts, his further explanations in the letters are virtually essential to an understanding of how he can identify the rhythm as 'the nearest to the rhythm of prose, that is the native and natural rhythm of speech, the least forced, the most *rhetorical* and emphatic of all possible rhythms,' while at the same time he prefaces the text of *Spelt from Sybil's Leaves* with the declaration that its reading should be 'poetical (not *rhetorical*)' (LI 46, 246; my emphases). Furthermore, only by putting together various of his communications does the importance that Hopkins attaches to phonetic quantity in sprung rhythm verse become clear: in particular, an 1877 letter to Bridges invoking Milton's attention to quantity (LI 44–6); an 1880 letter to Dixon on the nature of quantity in English that contrasts it with the Latin and Greek (LII 40–1); and an 1883 discussion with Patmore of the relationship of quantity to stress in English (LIII 329). The impressively consistent theoretical mosaic that the letters and prefaces form well substitutes for a single, extended explanation.

Alongside the documents assembled in the *Journals and Papers* and the collections of the correspondence, a last vital source for Hopkins's poetics is his annotations and markings of the manuscript texts of the poems, which Norman H. Mackenzie has edited in facsimile (MSI, MSII) and quite fully annotated in his standard edition of the *Poetical Works* (P). The major manuscripts contain the two vital explanations of sprung rhythm that I have mentioned, one of them heading up the first of the collections and another prefacing a text of *The Wreck of the Deutschland*. Preceding the texts of a number of the poems, Hopkins often supplies brief descriptions of the specific rhythms, which show him continually developing, varying, and refining his practice. For instance, he appends to the title of *Windhover* the note, 'Falling paeonic rhythm, sprung and outriding,' presenting his precise conception of the poem's metrics, which is hardly obvious. Additionally, he supplies many individual texts with diacritical marks, which often evidence more general features. In *Windhover*, he marks six double stresses, sixteen single stresses, two slurs, and nine 'outrides.' In line 10 of one of the three manuscript texts he writes 'AND' in capitals ('AND the fire that breaks from thee then'); in two others, instead, he puts the musical *sforzando* sign (>) over the same word. These notations, 'so much needed and yet so objectionable' (LI 215), while not always consistent between manuscripts in the symbols chosen, must be taken as generally faithful indications of the intention of an aurally acute, highly learned, skilled, and punctilious poet. The marks and brief comments within the text provide major testimony to the poet's linguistic and poetic ideas.

The preoccupation of Hopkins and his friends with matters of prosody and all varieties of rhyme was rooted in their school and university training in classical poetry, which had remained dominant in literary study. Nineteenth-century students of Virgil and Pindar, as had been traditional for more than two millennia, began study with the metrical form, with conventional analyses of foot and line units. That approach implicitly predicates that rhythmic pattern rather than Aristotelian mimesis represents the beginning of poetic life. Beginning in the early twentieth century, however, as a consequence of declining interest in the classics, accompanied by increased preoccupation with Aristotle and with literary theory and vernacular literature, students characteristically have begun study of poetry with vernacular verse and its discursive content, with matters such as character and theme, not with prosody. Critics of metrical vernacular poetry now typically approach it as a connected series of grammatical statements shaped to an imposed metrical form that regulates and adorns it. From that point of view, it would seem that beginning with metrical form gives priority to subordinate sound over rich semantic meaning. Thus, the dominant sensibility of classical poetry and theory, which conditioned the understanding of all poetry for many or most through the nineteenth century and implicitly accorded to verbal sound a prior and positive value, was superseded. At the same time, even today, the testimony of numerous major poets ascribes a prior constitutive role in poetry to rhythmic sound. For instance, Robert Frost's singling out of the 'sound of sense' as the specifically poetic component, referring to the sounds of the not-quite-distinguishable words that penetrate a closed door, seems to have a similar point in mind. In chapter 5, I cite his and similar statements about verse sound by several other poets, as well as interesting concurrences of their ideas with those of certain prominent theoreticians.

A major source of the Greek and Latin emphasis on sound patterning was the very early classification of metrical art as music: verse was seen as verbal music, coordinate with pitched music. As O.B. Hardison Jr states in treating the traditional relationship of musical and metrical theory, 'music bequeaths to ancient prosody' the concept that 'art is not imitative but constitutive,' making 'possible the perception of realities that would be unknowable without it' (21). Metrical form traditionally is not simply a formal regulator of language that contains and abridges the verbal expression; it is the originary conveyor of *poetic* meaning. The focus of Hopkins and his friends on prosody reflects their conditioning in classical poetry, and also in Hopkins's case his immersion in it as professor of Latin and Greek. All four poets implicitly accepted the traditional view that metrics has a power to constitute *affective* meaning, but Hopkins went further than most who have assumed a special significance to poetry; rather than stopping at ascribing ineffability to the contribution of poetic artifice, he formulated a philosophical explanation of its contribution to meaning.

Today, the notion that the inscapes of spoken language – speech figures – may embody a significance that goes beyond that of logic and grammar perhaps seems like mystification. On the contrary, Hopkins's conception, as his writings elaborate, offers a coherent, if metaphysical, explanation of the transformative power that readers and theorists over time have found in poetry. One assumes that he only slowly developed his ideas of 'inscape.' His early study of sketching and painting under Ruskin's influence encouraged his intensive observations of nature, particularities of clouds, waves, leaves, and so on. So conditioned, his highly theoretical mind and training in philosophical idealism with Benjamin Jowett, T.H. Green, and Walter Pater, led him to postulate that external forms had a metaphysical counterpart, an inner form that he identified as inscape. Intricate authoritative support for his concept came to him in his discovery of John Duns Scotus's realist formulation of the concepts of 'formalities' and 'thisness.' After that discovery, says the poet, 'when I took in any inscape of the sky and sea I thought of Scotus' (J 221). He professes to have found 'peace' in the reasoning of the Doctor Subtilis, 'Of realty [reality] the rarest veined unraveller' (*Duns Scotus's Oxford*, 11–12), preferring him 'even' to Aristotle and a 'dozen Hegels' (LI 31).

That he could find a congenial basis for his concepts in the notoriously difficult Latin distinctions of the Scholastic logician is a testimony to Hopkins's own learning and acuity. Of course, Scotus's association with Oxford and his Catholicism would have made his thinking attractive to the poet, but it would be a mistake to attribute Hopkins's adherence to his ideas to these factors. It is coincidental but nevertheless significant that in the same years that he was exploring Scotus's old volume on the *Sentences*, Charles Sanders Peirce, by all odds America's premier philosopher and no Catholic, was finding in the same thinker such inspiration that he came to declare himself a 'Scotistic realist,' a term that would have applied well to Hopkins but to very few others in their (or our) world.

It is consistent with their common discipleship that Hopkins's broad concept of linguistic significance as embracing the 'inscape' of verbal sound is supported by Peirce's 'Semiotics' and his now widely accepted definition of the sign. Peirce sees the sign's significance as threefold. In addition to what he calls *symbols*, whose meaning language arbitrarily assigns, are *icons* and *indexes*, which have non-arbitrary existential relationships with their objects: icons have resemblance, indexes direct connection. Of immediate relevance here are speech sounds, which we may see as phonetic icons of feeling, rather than merely bearers of the conventional lexical meanings that are assigned to words. Peirce explains the significance of the icon as being, to quote him, its embodiment of 'what it represents and for the mind that interprets it as such, by virtue of being an immediate image ... which belongs to it in itself as a sensible object.' On the most elementary level, a picture of a banana is an icon representing a banana. More subtly, we might instance as relevant to Hopkins's idea of the meaning of poetic sound, Peirce's attribution of iconic value to music: 'The performance of a piece of concerted music is a sign. It conveys, and is intended to convey the composer's musical ideas' (vol. 4, 1933; for more extended citation, see J. Wimsatt 1994, n.18). The music is an icon that, by virtue of the resemblance of the sounds to the composer's ideas, has a direct relationship to its object; the arbitrary symbol does not have such a relationship.

Hopkins's discussion in 'Poetry and Verse' presents verse as a major but not essential assistant to the poetic operation; the patterns of verse are finally ancillary to the pattern of speech sound. He did not change this idea; if anything he broadened it. Thus, in a late letter he asserts that the speaking voice potentially can produce effects superior to those of pitched music. He tells his younger brother Everard that just as 'prose, though commonly less beautiful than verse and debarred from its symmetrical beauties, has at least possible to it, effects more beautiful than any verse can attain, so perhaps the inflections and intonations of the speaking voice may give effects more beautiful than any attainable by the fixed pitches of music' (LIV 220). At the same time, the poet's description of music in his lecture notes on verse asserts an interesting parallel between verbal and pitched music, both based on 'vocal utterance': just as verse is 'the recasting of speech into sound-words, sound-clauses, and sound-sentences,' so 'music is the recasting of speech used in a wide sense, of vocal utterance, into words, clauses, and sentences of pitched sounds ... The musical syllable is the note, the musical foot or word [is] the bar ... the passage or melody down to the cadence [is] the sentence, the movement [is] the paragraph, the piece [is] the discourse' (J 273). To this way of thinking, one gathers, the function of both kinds of patterned sound, verbal and pitched, is to facilitate the detachment of the *speech* figure, and artful speech conceivably can do it even without depending on repetitions.

While Hopkins's subordination of both verse and pitched music to speech and the parallels he finds between the divisions of musical and the poetic texts are hardly standard theory, his deep experience with classical Greek and its intrinsic element of pitch, along with the originality of his thinking, help to validate his assertions. Linguistic pitch, he asserts to Everard, made Greek lyric poems into pitched songs: 'The Greeks carried lyric to its highest perfection in Pindar and the tragic choruses, but what was this lyric? not spoken lyric at all, but song; poetry written neither to be recited nor chanted even nor even sung to a transferable tune but each piece of itself a song' (LIV 220–1). Poetry for Pindar was pitched music – in the dramatic choruses, music timed to dance rhythm.

The Hopkinses were an artistic family; father, mother, brothers, sisters, uncles, and aunts painted, sketched, wrote poetry, and played and composed music. As a young man, Gerard had aspirations to become an artist; two of his brothers, Arthur and Everard, eventually painted and sketched professionally. His sister Grace similarly became a serious, though not professional, musician and composer, but it seems that it was only late that he developed his special love for music. His attachment was such that sometimes it became even stronger than his attachment to poetry. In 1881 he writes to Bridges that 'Every impulse and spring of art seems to have died in me, except for music' (LI 124). It is indicative of his confidence in his natural artistic competence that, despite minimal musical training, he freely speculated on technical matters with experts and ambitiously composed settings for poems of Shakespeare, for Greek and Latin poems, and poems of his friends. Eugene Hollahan is unnecessarily, and perhaps unwarrantedly, harsh in dismissing the poet's 'occasional pretensions to musical genius.' Though Hopkins freely discussed advanced concepts, he never claimed 'genius' (160–1; cf. J. Stevens).

Some of Hopkins's musical compositions are extant, but for his own verse only his patriotic tribute to England, 'What shall I do for the land that bred me?' (c. 1885). He intended to compose music for *The Leaden Echo and the Golden Echo* (1882) but evidently never got around to it. His remark about that work, 'I never did anything more musical,' applies to it in a special way. The repetitions and echoic effects of the poetic text itself make it musical in a manner that the poems that he says he set to music are not. The spoken text itself seems to sing. In a somewhat different way *Spelt from Sybil's Leaves* (1886) virtually chants itself. Hopkins indeed states that *Sybil's Leaves* 'essays effects almost musical,' and that it 'should be almost sung ... [being] most carefully timed in *tempo rubato*.' These late poems evidence his growing attachment to music. At the same time, his use of musical effects and descriptions for his verbal texts do not represent an attempt to transform the words into pitched music; he recognized that pitch has minor importance in modern European languages, and that even if the arts of poetry and music originally were the same, music's dependence on pitch had long divided them, though they remained close allies.

Hopkins knew well St Augustine's *De Musica*, which conveyed to the Middle Ages the ancient classification of poetry as one major kind of music: *verbal music,* coordinate with *pitched music.* Seeing poetry in this way is quite congenial with the poet's ideas and practice. Many of his theoretical statements treat poetry as verbal music, but as music either of speech or of verse, but not pitched. The triumph that Hopkins sees in sprung rhythm lies in its bringing together and harmonizing the two verbal musics, its combining of 'opposite and, one wd. have thought, incompatible excellences, markedness of rhythm – that is rhythm's self – and naturalness of expression' (LI 46). The measures of sprung rhythm are both uniform and flexible, accommodating equally regular verse rhythms and the irregular rhythms of speech.

This book extensively treats Hopkins's innovative ideas about verse and poetry, focusing on the quality of 'poeticalness,' which he first defined in 'Poetry and Verse,' and refined in his extensive subsequent writings. In explaining aspects of his ideas, he coined several new terms when the standard lexicon did not suffice. Most of these terms seem to me admirably chosen and in themselves revelatory. Thus, I use certain essential coinages as headings for subsequent chapters of this book. The best known and most important of them are 'sprung rhythm' and 'inscape,' the former denoting the verse system that Hopkins found to be well suited to achieving the ends of poetry, and the latter providing a label for the profound quality of poeticalness. Sprung rhythm as the poet defines it is especially fitting for his own practice of verse, but his analyses of it also offer important clarification of his broad concepts of poetic composition as applied to such central features as rhythm, speech, stress, verse, and phonetic quantity.

In Hopkins's poetics, rhythm is central, and it is logical that it provides the defining characteristic and the identifying term, 'rhythm,' for his innovative verse form. Sprung rhythm provides a meeting-place for speech music and verse music, and broad consideration of these two musics constitutes the first two chapters. He identifies *speech* rhythm specifically as the essential verbal element of poetry, so the first chapter, 'Sprung Rhythm: The Music of Speech,' takes up the most basic aspect of his poetics. It deals with the nature of speech music and how sprung rhythm can incorporate its irregularities into verse, which is by nature regular. The second chapter, 'Sprung Rhythm: The Music of Verse,' logically takes up the obverse problem, how a chosen verse form such as sprung rhythm can fit natural speech rhythms into its parameters. In Hopkins's concept, we find out from his late letters, the form, though typically verse, can even be prose. 'Lettering: Rhyme "Widely" Understood, the third chapter, expands the treatment of the form of verse in considering the important and historically controversial subject of the significance of phonetic sound repetition, including devices such as end-rhyme, alliteration, assonance, and other forms of 'sameness of sound between strong syllables in different words' (J 285). The poet's innovative term, 'lettering,' aptly points up this property, and his own exceptionally intensive uses of lettering, especially alliteration, ranks among the best empirical demonstrations in literature of its potential power and value.

The fourth chapter, '"Inscape" and Poetic Meaning,' gets back to the central concept of Hopkins's personal metaphysics. The chapter brings together his diverse uses of the term 'inscape,' together with any elucidating commentary, in order to clarify his applications of it to the 'scapes' of nature, to speech, and to his own poems and poetry in general. In his conception each sensory phenomenon has its own inscape, roughly 'inner pattern,' which apt and sufficient contemplation can reveal, at least in part. The prime aim of poetry is to reveal, and of verse to facilitate making known, the inscape of meaningful material speech, the power proper to humans that perhaps best embodies and reveals humanity's characteristic virtue. 'Poetry as the Language of the Body' is the fifth and last full chapter. The meaning 'over and above' the grammatical and logical that Hopkins sees as proper to poeticality enters the nascent poem prior to phonetic realization of the words and originates in bodily feelings and emotions manifested in the rhythms and sound patterns of the text. A like concept of a poem's origin is implicit in reports of numerous poets and explicit in the statements of prominent thinkers, notably Julia Kristeva and Friedrich Nietzsche. The accord of Hopkins's ideas with Kristeva's, which comes about because of their mutual privileging of sensory experience, is especially interesting, though, to be sure, the agreement is limited.

The conclusion, '"The Music of His Mind,"' adduces a Hopkins poem that muses about the architect of an ancient building as evidence that Hopkins, perhaps with some prompting from his tutor Walter Pater, saw music as the fundamental art, embracing, along with music, the works of architecture, sculpture, painting, and literature that successfully instress, bring out and support, the apposite inscape.

1 Sprung Rhythm: The Music of Speech

In a letter to Canon Dixon in 1878 Hopkins provides a short history and description of his sprung-rhythm verse. He recounts that after he became a Jesuit he refrained for seven years from composing poetry, 'as not belonging to my profession,' but when he mentioned to his rector his intense feelings about the sinking of the *Deutschland* off the English shore, the rector hinted indirectly that he might write a poem on the subject. Obviously, Hopkins was not slow to take the hint. It was then that he 'realised on paper' a 'new rhythm' whose 'echo' had been 'haunting' his ear for a long time. He describes the rhythm as consisting 'in scanning by accents or stresses alone, without any account of the number of syllables, so that a foot may be one strong syllable or it may be many light and one strong.' It is not 'altogether new,' he states, and he gives examples from nursery rhymes, '*Díng, dóng, béll,* etc.,' Shakespeare, and Campbell. But though he does not claim to have invented the rhythm, 'no one has professedly used it and made it the principle throughout' (LII 14–15).

Later in the letter he discusses Milton's counterpoint and how counterpoint, when it becomes dominant in a verse text, makes the rhythm 'sprung.' Here he provides his clearest explanation of what he means by a rhythm being 'sprung':

Milton is the great standard in the use of counterpoint. In *Paradise Lost* and *Regained,* in the last more freely, it being an advance in his art, he employs counterpoint more or less everywhere, markedly now and then; but the choruses of *Samson Agonistes* are in my judgment counterpointed throughout; that is each line (or nearly so) has two different coexisting scansions. But when you reach that point the secondary or 'mounted rhythm,' which is necessarily a sprung rhythm, overpowers the original or conventional one and then this becomes superfluous and may be got rid of; by taking that step you reach simple sprung rhythm. Milton must have known this but had reasons for not taking it. (LII 15)

For Hopkins the chief advantage of sprung rhythm lies in its bringing verse rhythms closer to natural speech rhythms than traditional verse systems usually allow. As I have indicated, for him human speech embodies pre-eminent values of language that are realized in poetry. In their status as language sounds, both prose and verse quintessentially are speech, and both can qualify as poetry. Furthermore, as he tells his brother Everard in an important late letter, prose conceivably can be more beautiful than verse, 'even though debarred of [verse's] symmetrical beauties.' Similarly, he continues, speech music may even be superior to pitched music: 'the inflections and intonations of the speaking voice may give effects more beautiful than any attainable by the fixed pitches of music' (LIV 220). The ideas expressed here are compatible with the much earlier essay 'Poetry and Verse' (J), in which the poet states that poetry's function is to detach the *inscape* of speech for contemplation, most commonly but not always through the repetitions of verse. The speech sound figure may be so distinctive and forceful that it does not need repeating to frame and detach it and thereby to convey the major values that the figure embodies.

Hopkins's various scattered statements about sprung rhythm, along with his comments about Walt Whitman's work, explain why he favours the 'logaoedic,' literally prose-poetic (LI 155–6), qualities of sprung rhythm. It minimizes the double danger confronting the poet: on the one hand, since the poetical is a particular quality of language inherent in speech, not a product of its external form, the regularities of verse form may obscure natural speech inflections; on the other hand, the rough rhythms of natural speech may inhibit perception and detachment of the speech figure. Consequently, a verse form that accommodates both the artificiality of verse and the roughness of natural speech rhythm, assuming that possibility, seems to Hopkins the most likely to reveal inscape. Thus, in the Preface to *The Wreck of the Deutschland* he describes sprung rhythm, in being freed from the usual regularities of uniform feet, as 'the most natural of things,' 'the rhythm of common speech and of written prose, when rhythm is perceived in them' (P 117).

The poet's own sprung-rhythm verse, with its intricate sound patterns, complex syntax, and neologisms, makes this assertion of naturalness and proselikeness seem paradoxical and his profession of poetic kinship with Whitman, the apostle of free verse, seem incongruous. But in his terms the claims make sense. He evidently pondered the American's work in some depth. 'I always knew in my heart,' he writes to Bridges, 'Walt Whitman's mind to be more like mine than any other man's' (adding righteously, 'As he is a very great scoundrel this is not a pleasant confession') (LI 155). The similarity that he identifies lies in the 'irregular rhythms' of the two poets, which Hopkins describes in terms of proselikeness. 'Extremes meet,' on the one hand, in Whitman's 'savage art and rhythm,' which 'is rhythmic prose and that only,' and, on the other, his own 'very highly wrought work.' Whitman's poetic composition, 'in its last ruggedness and decomposition into common prose, comes near the last elaboration of mine' (156–7).

In Hopkins's generally consistent usage, *prose* does not contrast with *poetry*. Moreover, to the poet's classically conditioned sensibility, prose does not suggest artlessness, though its rhythms are fundamentally more conformable to natural speech. Prose is under the aegis of the art of rhetoric. In a student essay he puts forward writings of Burke and Shelley's preface to *Adonais* as English models of 'noble and eloquent prose' (J 107). Later, as professor of classical languages, he goes beyond vernacular exemplars to find in classical theory his canons for prose, which notably prescribe a system of rhythmic *clausulae* – metrical feet – applied especially to sentence endings. He cites the dicta of Aristotle and Cicero, quoting the former's statement that oratory should have rhythm but not 'exact rhythm' and 'not metre (which would make it poetry).' By metre, Aristotle signifies verse lines, not the foot unit. He is thus allowing that while foot structures are often desirable in prose, especially for beginnings and endings, a speech should not be divisible into verse lines ('metres') so as to have regular rhythm throughout. Hopkins notes that the foot patterns that Aristotle prescribes for prose are the first and fourth paeons (a long and three shorts, three shorts and a long), neither of which makes metres (i.e., verse lines). He further calls to witness Cicero's recommendation of falling metre for Latin sentences; nevertheless, Hopkins observes, terminal short syllables 'will not suit with the final paeon' (J 275–6).

Other of Hopkins's statements about sprung rhythm supplement his Preface to *Deutschland*. Formulating a response to Bridges's queries about his rationale, he describes the rhythm as 'nearest to the rhythm of prose, that is the native and natural rhythm of speech, the least forced, the most rhetorical and emphatic of all speech rhythms.' The rhythm reconciles the two primary elements of poetic sound: natural speech and strong rhythm: 'Why do I employ sprung rhythm at all?' he asks rhetorically, responding that it is because it combines 'opposite, and one wd. have thought, incompatible excellences, markedness of rhythm ... and naturalness of expression' (LI 46). In sprung rhythm, then, two kinds of verbal music happily intersect: on the one hand, it has marked rhythm, requiring a clearly defined recurrence of stress, and on the other hand, it has naturalness, the stress patterns of natural speech.

Hopkins's prescription of 'naturalness of expression' thus does not call for artless use of language; rather, it requires expressive speech whose sounds fit in with the natural patterns of the physical world, what he would call its 'scapes.' Speech music involves, in the first place, the great variety of segmental phones, intonations, inflections, and emphases that common speech employs in a variable order and mix, while the main constituents of verse music are planned rhythmic repetitions of feet, lines, stanzas, and ordered sound sequences. Hopkins's theoretical writings indicate that it is in speech music, rather than verse music, that poetry's characteristic value lies, verse repetition being an instrument for manifesting the value. For him, the rhythm of speech unsegmented by verse is the rhythm of prose (which if properly artful *can* qualify as poetry). As I noted above, in his lecture notes for 'Rhythm and Other Structural Parts of Rhetoric – Verse' (to which 'Poetry and Verse' is appended in manuscript) Hopkins follows classical theory, notably Aristotle's *Rhetoric*, in treating 'prose' as artful, rhythmic speech. '*Metre*,' Hopkins comments, 'is the grouping of a *certain number* of feet ... in modern verse *a* verse means a complete metrical figure, a metrical unit, for as the foot is the rhythmic unit, which it repeats, so a verse is the metrical unit of repetition' (J 273). A *verse* in these terms can be a line or a stanza. He quotes the *Rhetoric*'s prescription of the proper rhythm for speech, rhythm neither exact nor without plan: 'Partial rhythm will be what we want' (275).

Aristotle rejects dactylic rhythm for prose as 'too solemn for speaking and needing music,' and iambic and trochaic 'for want of dignity.' He holds that the four-syllable paeon is properly popular with orators. The paeonic, Hopkins comments, is the only one of the various rhythms that Aristotle names '"which by itself does not make metre, so that it passes unnoticed the easiest"' (J 275–6). Hopkins remarks on the philosopher's explanation of the paeon's failure to make metre as a matter of proportion. If we count the long syllable as two units and the short as one, the dactyl and spondee have a proportion of one to one, while the iamb and trochee are one to two or two to one. These are properly metrical, but the paeon, with a proportion three to two or two to three, will not form a definite metre (J 275).

Hopkins's analysis is quite indicative for his concepts of sprung rhythm and of prose. He infers that Aristotle bases his recommendation of the paeon on 'the complexity of the [paeon's] ratio, which is hard to catch, and ... its length, which makes the longs and beats wide apart and so also hard to catch the particular rhythm of, though rhythmical' (J 276). This understanding provides a gloss to his statement to Bridges that sprung rhythm 'is the nearest to the rhythm of prose, that is the native and natural rhythm of speech' in combining 'markedness of rhythm ... and naturalness of expression' (LI 46). It seems likely that Aristotle's analysis of prose rhythm suggested to Hopkins that the poet can make 'rhythmical' verse more natural by varying the number of unstressed syllables, thereby making it 'hard to catch the particular rhythm.'

Aristotle's finding the paeon appropriate for prose rhythm evokes both Hopkins's professed use of the paeon in his sprung-rhythm verse, and his assertion of the proselikeness of sprung rhythm. However, though the poet embraces the paeon, neither in his discussion of sprung rhythm nor in his practice does the foot dominate. In his Preface he says that the sprung rhythm foot has 'one stress, which falls on the only syllable, if there is only one, or, if there are more ... on the first, and so gives rise to four sorts of feet, a monosyllable and the so-called accentual Trochee, Dactyl, and the First Paeon. And there will be four corresponding natural rhythms; but nominally the feet are mixed and any one may follow any other. And hence Sprung Rhythm differs from Running Rhythm [common verse rhythm such as the iambic] in having or being only one nominal rhythm, a mixed or "logaoedic" one, instead of three, but on the other hand in having twice the flexibility of foot, so that any two stresses may follow one another running or be divided by one, two, or three slack syllables' (P 116). He presents the paeon here, then, not as the dominant foot, but rather as a possibility. At the same time, in his annotations of specific poems, he specifically indicates that the paeon marks the rhythm of three of his best mature short poems: *The Windhover* is in 'falling paeonic rhy[th]m' (P 376); *Pied Beauty* in 'sprung paeonic rhythm' (P 384); and *The Caged Skylark* in 'falling paeonic rhythm, sprung and outriding' (P 386). A number of their feet are, in fact, paeons, but most consist of three syllables or less, so the meaning of the notations is a matter for speculation: they may indicate isochronous foot timing with the paeon a usual syllable limit. He does not mention a dominant foot pattern for his other sprung rhythm works. A final interesting reference to the paeon is the poet's comment to Dixon that 'paeons (three short syllables and a long or three slacks and one stressy) are regular in sprung rhythm, but in common rhythm can occur only by licence.' He adds that in sprung rhythm even longer feet than the paeon are 'allowed for special rhythmic effects' (LII, 39).

It is notable, furthermore, that Hopkins's specific examples of sprung rhythm more often point up use of monosyllabic rather than four-syllable feet. In his Preface he states that sprung rhythm occurs in old 'nursery rhymes, weather saws, and so on' (P 117), because in the course of time 'the terminations having dropped off ... the stresses come together and so the rhythm is sprung.' Accordingly, writing to Dixon, he cites particularly nursery rhymes with monosyllabic feet, such as '*Díng, dóng, béll*' and '*óne, twó*, Búckle my shoe'; similarly, the notable feet in his other examples, from Campbell and Shakespeare, have but one strong syllable (LII 15). With reference to his own verse he asks Bridges, 'for why, if it is forcible in prose to say "lashed: rod," am I obliged to weaken this in verse ... into "láshed birch ród" or something?' (LI 46; cf. *Deutschland*, line 10). His markings of stress in the manuscripts also very often indicate monosyllabic feet.

The proselikeness of sprung rhythm, then, lies in its free mixing of foot types, the range of one to four-syllable feet producing both adjacent and widely separated stresses, which tend to obscure the underlying regularity of the rhythm. Hopkins also recommends running the feet over the line ends, further concealing the divisions and conducing to 'naturalness of expression.' He emphasizes that the naturalness results from a carefully planned *rhythm*. It is not laxity in timing or inattention to syntax that gives rise to the proselikeness of his sprung rhythm. With reference to Bridges's analysis of *The Leaden Echo and the Golden Echo*, while admitting that his mind is like Whitman's, he also avers that the common similarity of their verse to prose comes from different directions: while Whitman's rhythm verges on 'decomposition into common prose,' his own is 'very highly wrought. The long lines are not rhythm run to seed: everything is weighed and timed in them.' Hopkins allies the rhythm of *Echoes* with that 'of Greek tragic choruses or of Pindar, which is pure sprung rhythm.' He adds, too, that his 'remarks are not meant to run down Whitman,' that the American *intends* 'a "savage" art and rhythm' (LI 157). He clearly admired Whitman's innovative art, if not his way of life.

For Hopkins, speech sound is the special locus of the poetic and thereby is a major source of language significance. His view contrasts with much of modern language theory. For Ferdinand de Saussure's 'Semiology,' notably and influentially, speech sound has two aspects, *langue* and *parole*, but only *langue* belongs to the language system. Sound *contrasts*, not sound qualities, comprise the whole of *langue*, while *parole* comprises all of vocal presentation apart from the sound contrasts. Saussure is quite categorical in excluding sound qualities from *langue*: 'The executive side of [the speech circuit] plays no part [in *langue*], for execution [i.e., *parole*] is never carried out by the collectivity: it is always individual, and the individual is always master of it' (1986, §30). The purview of *langue* is determined by a system of negative contrasts of distinctive sound features that differentiate language meanings, both grammatical and lexical. The positive values of linguistic sound, under the purview of *parole*, have no value in themselves for systematic language meaning. *Parole* is 'always individual,' that is, it lacks norms, and whatever significance it has is in control of the speaker. It is not part of the system of *langue*.

As a student of classical languages and philosophy, Hopkins was very interested in language theory. How he might have responded to Saussure, had he lived into the twentieth century, is, of course, uncertain. Nevertheless, while for semiology all the meanings of *langue* are determined by negative contrasts, the poet treats positive qualities of speech sound, which the Swiss linguist classes as *parole* rather than *langue*, as being at the heart of characteristically poetic significance; these are not, or according to Hopkins should not be, strictly dependent on the speaker. He declares to Everard that 'the inflections and intonations of the speaking voice' might produce 'effects more beautiful' than those of pitched music, conceiving these effects as predictably produced when a poetical work is properly presented; but at the same time he grants that fixing norms for oral presentation poses a major practical problem. At one time, as in classical Greece, poetry was an oral art; it began with speech. Now it 'has this great difficulty, that the art depends entirely on living tradition. The phonograph may give us one, but hitherto there could be no record of fine spoken utterance' (LIV 220).

Hopkins's idea of employing exemplary phonographic recordings to show how each poetical work should be read implies clearly that the poet can and should determine aspects of oral presentation of a poetic work beyond those fixed by the present graphic code. His concept of the recordings, which would standardize the oral reading of a text, recalls his extensive use of superscripts and of notations sometimes borrowed from music to show the manner in which his poems, 'less to be read than heard' (LI 46), should be stressed and accented. He uses the markings more extensively in later texts than in earlier ones; after he began his sprung-rhythm work, he consistently felt their need and increasingly realized that he could not rely on his readers to read his poems properly without them. The markings, he laments to Bridges, are 'so much needed and yet so objectionable' (LI 215). His groping for an effective marking code for his verse, a standard notation for oral presentation, effectively implies that features of segmental sound, of intonation and emphasis, have correct and incorrect forms for a poem, *systematic* complexities beyond contrastive analysis, which the existing graphic system – involving limited alphabetic orthography, punctuation, and diacritics – has not developed a way of showing. These aspects of speech especially communicate significance, 'over and above' logical sense, which is at the heart of his – and he would say all – lyric poetry. His concept agrees significantly with Dwight Bolinger's statement in his standard study of intonation, 'There are rules, but they respond to *feeling* more directly than does any other well-systematized part of spoken language' (1986, viii; my emphasis). The positive significances of language sound are affective ones. They respond to feeling more directly, and implicate a wide spectrum of emotional and sensuous experience. It seems consistent with Hopkins's concept of poetical meaning 'over and above' the logical to infer, furthermore, that such linguistic meaning can extend well beyond intonation and stress to include all aspects of speech sound.

Hopkins suggests recordings to obviate the innate deficiencies of the present graphic system – especially for poetry – by providing a model that will serve the function that the conventions of musical notation supply for pitched music. Semiology holds that *parole* is 'an individual's use of the code provided by the language [*langue*] in order to express his own thought' (Saussure §30), while Hopkins's search for effective diacritical markings to direct reading of his poems implicitly suggests that a shared *system* for expressive features is a proper linguistic aspect of human speech and a necessary part of a poem's spoken performance. What is important in his view is communication of the feeling in the poetic work and only secondarily the reciter's own feeling.

The poet's further statement to Everard merits quoting in full, notably for its identification of lyric poetry with speech, providing the ideal locus for 'fine spoken utterance': 'In drama the fine spoken utterance has been cultivated and a tradition established, but everything is most highly wrought and furthest developed where it is cultivated by itself;

fine utterance then will not be best developed in the drama, where gesture and action generally are to play a great part too; it must be developed in recited lyric.' Hopkins then speaks of the nature of the lyric in tonal languages like classical Greek, which contrasts to that in non-tonal languages like English: 'Now hitherto this has not been done. The Greeks carried lyric to its highest perfection in Pindar and the tragic choruses, but what was this lyric? not a spoken lyric at all, but song; poetry neither to be recited nor chanted nor even sung to a transferable tune but each piece itself a song.' The speech-sound patterns of English lyrics, properly fixed and learned, have potential to make a 'lovely art' of 'incalculable effect': 'The same remark then as above recurs: the natural performance and delivery belonging properly to lyric poetry, which is speech, has not been enough cultivated, and should be. When perform-ers were trained to do it (it needs the rarest gifts) and audiences to appreciate it it would be, I am persuaded, a lovely art. Incalculable effect could be produced by the delivery of Wordsworth's *Margaret* ('Where art thou, my beloved son?' – do you know it?) With the aid of a phonograph each phrase could be fixed and learnt by heart like a song' (LIV 220–1). He is calling for a standard that can be specified for all performances of a poem. Just as songs have music based on a shared system of expressive sound for which the performances will vary, so poems have, beyond the grammatical and logical meaning of *langue*, a shared base of expressive and affective meaning.

Hopkins's assertion of the naturalness proper to a poem's perfor-mance evokes the terminology he uses in describing sprung rhythm: 'the most natural of things' (P 117), 'the native and natural rhythm of speech' (LI 46). Because of such statements, his formulation of sprung rhythm has commonly been thought, following Father Ong's analysis, to call for ordinary linguistic intonation (1949); but this is not his concept of the rhythm, as I discuss at more length in the next chapter, 'Sprung Rhythm: The Music of Verse.' In promoting exemplary recordings in-stead of celebrating individuality, he is calling for the establishment of standards for oral reading of lyric poetry such as, he believes, already had been established in drama and that once prevailed in lyric poetry before the custom of private reading developed. Such norms would order the system of expressive speech sound beyond the capabilities of the present graphic system.

Poetry for Hopkins is speech, but not compulsorily verse. Speech sound, not lexical and grammatical meaning, is the main grounding for poetry's peculiar value, as he repetitively emphasizes in his piece, 'Poetry and Verse': '*Poetry is speech* framed for contemplation of the mind by the way of hearing or *speech* framed to be heard for its own sake and interest even over and above its interest of meaning.' Poetry is 'only employed to carry the inscape of *speech*.' It is '*speech* wholly or partially repeating some kind of figure which is over and above meaning' (J 289–90; my emphases). For Hopkins, the inscape of the speech figure detached from particular wording carries poetry's proper significance. Such significance clearly is related to the conviction of many that literature has special meaning beyond and preceding its specific lexical sense, what Wallace Stevens calls 'imaginative or emotional meanings' and many others denominate by similarly affective terms such as 'aesthetic' or 'musical.'

Analysis of the phonetic contrasts that affect lexical meanings is central in current study of language sound, phonology. These contrasts, to which usage has arbitrarily assigned meanings – one sound contrast is as effective as another – are tacitly assumed to embrace the whole purview of systematic language meaning. At the same time, some prominent linguists and semioticians have dissented, finding that the significance of language and language sound goes beyond that of the arbitrary contrasts, which identify 'grammatical, historical, and logical' meanings. Important scholars from the past century, such as Otto Jespersen and Roman Jakobson, have called to witness representational relationships, by which the sound directly represents word meanings, positive elements that can fortify and deepen lexical sense. Jakobson's ideas on speech sound conform in important ways with those of Hopkins, but the specifics, such as onomatopoeia, that he adduces in his comprehensive treatment of these relationships provide a disappointing harvest (1988). These effects, while certainly well founded, are ad hoc and quite sporadic. More fruitful is the approach of the semiotician Julia Kristeva, who in many ways builds on Jakobson's linguistic insights, notably his privileging of speech sound. Unlike her mentor, however, she views language sound as a signifier independent of lexical meaning, taking exception to the adoption by linguistics of a 'logical, normative basis for the speaking subject' and an 'object of study' that does not assimilate the 'pre- and trans-logical rhythm' of spoken language: 'The speech practice that should be [linguistics'] object is one in which signified structure (sign, syntax, signification) is defined within boundaries that can be shifted by the advent of a semiotic rhythm that no system of linguistic communication has yet been able to assimilate. It would deflect linguistics toward a consideration of language as articulation of a heterogeneous process, with the speaking subject leaving its imprint on the dialectic between articulation and process. In short, this would establish *poetic language* as the object of linguistics' attention in its pursuit of truth in language' (1980, 24–5). The poetic element in language has an important part in 'truth in language.' In lyric poetry the 'speaking subject' is the poet or his surrogate reader.

Kristeva particularly values Jakobson's understanding of 'poetic language,' which he presents as one major feature of linguistic meaning (Jakobson 1987, 66–7). She futher singles out for special praise the linguistic sensitivity of his oral performance of the poetry of Mayakovsky and Khlebnikov. Her description indicates that he treats the original performances of the poets as exemplary, really as part of the works. She describes Jakobson's 'imitating their voices, with the lively rhythmic accents, thrust out throat and fully militant tone of the first; and the softly whispered words, sustained swishing and whistling sounds, vocalizations of the disintegrating voyage toward the mother constituted by the "trans-mental" ... language of the second.' She quotes Mayakovsky's narration of his process of poetic composition in which he asserts the priority of rhythm, 'resounding through the whole thing' (Kristeva 27–9). Jakobson's respectful imitation of the poet's speaking voice in his recitations reflects an attitude very like what Hopkins indicates in advocating exemplary recordings, with which he proposes to preserve a proper oral presentation of specific poems. He would have valued Mayakovsky's and Khlebnikov's performances together with Jakobson's simulation of them.

Application of Kristeva's ideas about language, which see speech practice as a proper object of linguistics and poetry as a crown of language significance rather than the product of 'a secondary modeling system,' as literary theoreticians such as Yuri Lotman and William Wimsatt have postulated, is not confined to the ethical-political argument to which she applies it. Her theory suggests treating language as innately dialogic, with rhythm and other sound features carrying complexities of meaning that may conflict with the logic of the verbal statement, thereby presenting a 'contest between rhythm and sign system' (Kristeva 34). More broadly, it conforms well to Hopkins's implicit concept of the music of speech sound as an overriding constitutive force in language meaning. I treat Kristeva's relevance to Hopkins further in chapter 5.

George Steiner is another important thinker who, coming at the problem from a different direction, finds current linguistics, represented by Noam Chomsky's powerfully influential generative theory of language, quite imperfect, especially in its ignoring of the poetic aspect. In his encyclopedic treatment of translation, *After Babel*, he observes: 'Natural language is local, mobile, and pluralistic in relation to even the simplest acts of reference' (214), asserting that the nuances of poetry are part of the continuum of natural language meaning, not a product of a secondary system. Referring to the salient problem of poetic translation, he states, 'To know more of language and of translation we must pass from the "deep structures" of transformational grammar to the deeper structure of the poet' (114).

Despite the importance of sound to translation of verse especially, in his study Steiner only intermittently treats the phonic aspect as an independent element of meaning. His discussion of Dadaist attempts at 'sound-poetry,' notably by Hugo Ball, leads in that direction (1985, 191–8). Ball's account of his compositional process evokes the testimony of diverse poets who assert the priority of sound and rhythm in the creation and meaning of a work, discussed in chapter 5 below. Ball states, "'I do not know whence came the inspiration for the cadence. But I began to chant my rows of vowels in the manner of liturgical plain song ... For a moment it seemed to me as if the pale, distraught face of a young boy had emerged from my cubist mask ... Before speaking the lines, I had read out a few programmatic words. In this kind of "sound-poetry" ... one relinquishes – lock, stock, and barrel – the language which journalism has polluted and made impossible. You withdraw into the inmost alchemy of the word'" (quoted in Steiner 1985, 203–4).

Ball searches for a new idiosyncratic vocabulary in manipulation of sound. Hopkins's verse likewise works towards a renewal of language, with sound as the central feature, but *not*, as with Dadaists like Ball, by discarding linguistic meaning and creating language anew, but instead by 'heightening ... the current language.' Sound carries major independent significance, but alongside – or underneath – verbal sense. Moreover, Hopkins would not have agreed with the vague mysticism of Ball's concepts. As a Jesuit priest, he indeed perceived the world in ultimately spiritual terms, but he was a philosopher-poet and a theoretician who was not drawn to enigmatic formulations. His concepts do accord with the conviction of many, both Christians and non-Christians, that literature has special significance beyond its logical word sense, the ':imaginative or emotional meanings' that Wallace Stevens evokes and others have described in similarly affective terms. The Romantics' concept of poetry assumes such ineffable meaning, but Hopkins's poetics apparently draws little directly from them. Rather, he worked out original explanations, using fresh terms and pointing mainly to features of verbal speech for the common perception that poetry has special meaning.

The current success of semiology has undercut the force of the once-standard position that a poet's work is in some way charged with – and characterized by – a special significance beyond its lexical sense. Thus, a writer like Octavio Paz is led to doubt his innate conviction that sound and sense are allied metaphysically:

'It has always been believed that the relation between sound and meaning appertained not only to the natural order but also to the supernatural; they were inseparable and the tie that joined them was indissoluble. The idea presents itself spontaneously to the understanding ... I confess that it is only with great antipathy that I accept (provisionally) the fact that the relation between sound and meaning, as Ferdinand de Saussure and his disciples maintain, is the result of an arbitrary convention. My misgivings are natural: poetry is born of the age-old magic belief in the identity of the word and what it names.' (quoted in Heaney, 'Drag' 14)

Paz associates his instinctive conviction about language with 'age-old magic,' while Heaney, in quoting Paz, registers his continued faith in 'those ghostlier demarcations and keener sounds of the ideal poetic order' ('Drag' 14). 'Magic' and 'ghostlier' reflect the ineffability that poets and sensitive readers have often assigned to specifically poetic meaning, though they also suggest vagueness and insubstantiality. Hopkins was more circumstantial in explaining the significances that go beyond those of logic and grammar. In his early diary, he had considered a simple sound-meaning relationship, asserting that the 'onomatopoetic theory of language had not had a fair chance' (J 5), and even later in life he doubtless would have been sympathetic to Jakobson's essay, 'The Spell of Speech Sounds,' which explores ways in which language sound imitates verbal sense, a positive phonetic value, not merely a negative one.

But Hopkins's mature poetics of sound finds a much more potent and pervasive value in speech sound than direct sound symbolism. He locates it in the 'inscape' of the utterance, based on the pattern of its sounds, in the speech music that poetry isolates for contemplation. For him language sound has *positive* linguistic value that is not a product of a secondary system, but a primary, fundamental significance realized most fully in poetry. His concept of language and poetry agrees in important ways with that of Jakobson, who was a prime theorist and spokesman for the ideas developed in the first half of the twentieth century by the Russian formalists and then in the Prague Linguistic Circle.

The 1935 'programmatic statement' of the Prague Circle, signed by Jakobson and other prominent members, declares that 'Only poetry ... enables us to experience the *art of speech in its totality*' (Erlich 157; my emphasis). The assumption that poetry represents the 'art of speech' is basic to Jakobson's concept of poetry and of language as speech and of course is quite consonant with the much earlier dictum of Hopkins that poetry is speech 'framed to be heard for its own sake' ('Poetry and Verse'). Jakobson early incorporated linguistics and poetics into semiotics, the science of signs, and he was also instrumental in recognizing 'distinctive features' as a basis for analysing language. But he did not believe that the sound symbolism negatively identified by distinctive features represented the only linguistic value of language sound. In responding to the such exclusive valorization, while readily granting the autonomous role of 'distinctive features,' he asserts that at the same time 'the linguist cannot ignore any aspect of language: the *whole* of the *speech* sound is an artifact made for the aims of language. No phase of the speech sound can be dismissed by the investigator as quasi-irrelevant' (Jakobson and Waugh, 233). The implicit inclusion of poetry in this declaration is consistent with Jakobson's concept of the integral part of the poetic in language, and with his idea of language itself.

Quite apart from the theories of linguists, critics of Hopkins's own verse have often remarked on the materiality or opacity of its sounds. Geoffrey Hartman speaks of Hopkins's direct engagement with 'the materiality of language' (1970, 243). He notes the accord of I.A. Richards, William Empson, and F.R. Leavis in finding that Hopkins's 'strength was bound up with the *immediacy of his relation to words*'; for them, 'he seemed to fulfill the dream that poetry was language speaking about itself, language uttering complex words that were meanings as words' (231; my emphasis). He concludes that 'Language, through him, is again part of the body of things, if not of its very essence' (244).

Through much of the twentieth century and notably in Eastern Europe, linguists and semioticians regularly asserted a positive significance of sound in language. Cary Plotkin in his book on Hopkins's 'poetic language' invokes the Eastern European linguists in finding an essential similarity between their ideas and the poet's: 'The priority that Hopkins grants to language itself and particularly to the element of sound in language seems to confirm in anticipation, or at least to prefigure, the work of later theoreticians of poetics who trace their positions back to the Prague Linguistic Circle. The deautomatizing or actualizing of linguistic structures that the Prague theorists and before them the Russian theorists had isolated as a constitutive element seems nowhere in English literature prior to the present century more explicitly borne out than in Hopkins' poems and writing on poetry' (8; cf. Erlich 180–6). Language sound, Plotkin indicates, is the key element in this 'actualizing': 'The density of his poetic language ... seems to reveal a new linguistic connection between words, both in their depth and in their surfaces,' the connections being 'almost always signaled, declared, uttered by sound' (122).

Interestingly, later in his study Plotkin notes Gérard Genette's treatment of Plato's ideas of language sound and the view that 'Plato recognizes in sound symbolism a way out of the circularity of trying to establish propriety in words by reference to other words. What matters ... is not the propriety of words but the propriety of sounds. It seems possible that Plato, contrary to the usual assumption that he denigrates the Cratylist view that words are direct signifiers, may actually be a partisan of Cratylus, believing in a "truth of *sounds* that language *betrays*"' (Plotkin 139). Plotkin does not explore further implications for Hopkins's theory, but such a view might allow that the semiotic function of the sounds is not simply to reinforce or deepen lexical meanings but has priority in the whole scope of linguistic significance. A similar view of poetic language may explain the enigma of Hopkins's idea that poeticality resides in speech figures that have significance 'over and above ... logical meaning.'

After his very early diary note, 'I think the onomatopoetic theory [of language origin] has not had a fair chance' (1863), Hopkins tacitly abandons consideration of direct sound symbolism. When he again deals importantly with language sound in his papers, it is to declare its central role in poetic expression. The *inscape* of speech, of the sounds of spoken language, he has come to believe, embody the quality of poeticalness. But that bare determination, expressed confidently in his resourceful personal idiom, still leaves us far from understanding in what element or aspect of the poetry we might isolate the speech figure. Wherein lies this inscape underlying speech patterns that is the locus of poetry's special value? Though important scholars have put forward uncomplicated definitions, the concept of inscape is not simply explained in the way 'onomatopoeia' or 'sound symbolism' are, nor is it a simple concept. As I quoted more fully above, Hillis Miller asserts that Hopkins's 'inscape of verse is a pattern of sound which may be repeated' (1966, 94), and Maria Lichtman, inspired in part by Miller, defines it briefly as 'parallelism' (5, 8, passim). These seem straightforward explanations, but they involve devices rather than concepts. Furthermore, while parallels, say, of sound or of grammar, may help the reader to detach an inscape, they lead precisely to the kind of endless loop that Miller would identify in Hopkins's theory of verse: 'Different modes of echoing means that all words taken together form an elaborate system of interrelated reverberations. But in defining poetry in this way Hopkins has cut it off from the poet and from nature' (Miller 1966, 96). But Hopkins says that the inscape is found in the speech figure, which may be detached for 'contemplation,' not that it is directly understood by means of repetition. I will assert a more complex and philosophically satisfactory explanation of inscape in chapter 4. For now I rely on the obvious sense, 'inner landscape,' to serve as a tentative definition.

Hopkins's descriptions suggest that one feature of spoken language that has particular relevance to poetic significance is its innate and authentic attachment to time and place. Hopkins wants the sound figures of verse to reproduce the 'native and natural rhythm of speech,' wording that evokes statements of various other poet-theorists. For one it suggests Wordsworth's intention of presenting his *Lyrical Ballads* 'in a selection of language really used by men.' One fundamental difference is that Hopkins focuses explicitly on speech sound, while Wordsworth's preface suggests that verse expression should be more like unadorned prose. Hopkins, in fact, in a short undergraduate essay, 'Poetic Diction' (1865), had found deficient Wordsworth's view that 'The most interesting parts of the best poems will be found to be strictly the language of prose when prose is well written' (J 84). While this formula may have served as a healthy corrective, he states, the artifice of verse usually is needed – notably, its parallelisms. Later, when Hopkins had fixed emphatically on the central role of sound figures in poetry, he acknowledges explicitly the potential of artful prose, but he does not find the poetical simply in prose that is 'well written.'

Other major poets are like Hopkins in demanding for poetry the common *rhythms* of speech. Quite compatible with Hopkins's description is Robert Frost's identifying the 'best place to get the abstract sound of sense is from behind a door that cuts off the words' (58–9). For Frost the 'the sound of sense' comes from the intonations, emphases, and audible letter sounds of speech; the 'sense,' then, is not the logical meanings generated by the sound contrasts, but the affective component of a speech. T.S. Eliot's formulation of the 'music of poetry' suggests Hopkins's aspiration to reproduce 'rhythms of speech' that are both 'natural' and 'native.' 'The music of poetry,' says Eliot, 'must be latent in the common speech of the *time*. And that means it must also be latent in the common speech of the poet's *place*' (1942, 17; his emphases). Hopkins's notebooks and letters correspondingly show a lively sensitivity to localisms, found in turn in the diction and idiomatic expressions in his verse. Seamus Heaney is attracted specifically to the evocation of regional speech in Hopkins's verse. He associates his own early poetry with Hopkins's 'bumpy alliterating music ... reporting sounds and ricocheting consonants,' discerning in these the sounds of the English of his Ireland. He sees 'the heavily accented consonantal noise of Hopkins' poetic voice' as being of a piece with 'the peculiar regional characteristics of a Northern Ireland accent' (1980, 44).

Hopkins, Eliot, and Heaney all emphasize the importance of time and place in the poet's verse sounds. Particularly in the light of Hopkins's interests in language, dialect usage and dialect poetry seem likely factors to isolate what he conceives to be the 'poetical' quality. He contributed substantially to Joseph Wright's *English Dialect Dictionary*, and in his diaries he records dialect words and phrases that he heard in his travels: the Lancashire name for rose bush, 'Virgin's Briar (they says breer),' the Manx name for cormorants, 'Black Divers.' He could find the popular word for kestrel, 'windhover,' in Richard Chevenix Trench's *On the Study of Words*, along with Trench's comment on the descriptive felicity of the term for the bird's 'hanging poised in the air, before it swoops' (Milroy 80–2). Milroy's listing of Hopkins's use of rare and non-standard words includes numerous examples of local usages that reflect the poet's experiences in rural England, Wales, and Ireland (232–48). As with the series of words recorded in the diaries, his interest in 'native' words and expressions fixes largely on their sounds.

Hopkins, nevertheless, is not a particular admirer of dialect poetry because of its most obvious qualities. In an extended discussion with Bridges of the Dorset dialect poetry of William Barnes, who is mainly known today as an influence on Hardy's Wessex stories, he formulates a principle that poetry should represent the 'current language heightened.' Yet it is telling that Hopkins defends Barnes's verse, which Bridges had disparaged, not on the basis of any 'native and natural' strength in dialect usage, but rather for rhythmic qualities not especially associated with dialect peculiarities. He finds Barnes's dialect poems better poetically than those of Robert Burns *because* they are more readily translatable into standard English: 'A proof of their excellence is that you may translate them and they are nearly as good – I say nearly, because if the dialect plays any lawful part in the effect they ought to lose something in losing that. Now Burns loses prodigiously by translation' (LI 87).

Hopkins at this point treats Bridges to a broader, not entirely convincing, meditation on dialect practice, which is notable for the limitations he places on its role in creating an authentic 'instress': 'I think the use of dialect a sort of unfair play, giving, as you say, "a peculiar but shortlived charm," setting off for instance a Scotch or Lancashire joke which in standard English comes to nothing. But its lawful charm and use I take to be this, that it sort of guarantees the spontaneousness of the thought ... as coming from nature and not from books and education.' In Barnes's work the use of dialect 'narrows his field' but 'heightens his effects.' Hopkins's analysis of Burns and of the strength of dialect use is not especially compelling, but his further discussion of the instress characteristic of Dorset is appealing and it is enlightening for his concept. Instress comparable to that in Barnes's poetry, he asserts, characterizes diverse phenomena: non-dialect songs and verse of southwest England, the regional landscapes, and the pleasant odours of the local flora: 'His poems use to charm me also by their Westcountry "instress," a most peculiar product of England, which I associate with airs like Weeping Winefred, Polly Oliver, or Poor Mary Ann, with Herrick and Herbert, with the Worcestershire, Herefordshire, and Welsh landscape, and above all with the smell of oxeyes and applelofts: this instress is helped by particular rhythms and these Barnes employs; as, I remember, in "Linden Ore" and a thing with a refrain like "Alive in the Spring"' (LI 88). The instress, which sustains inscape, he finds manifested synaesthetically in a variety of sensory experiences.

Hopkins here is recalling Barnes from early contact with his verse, but six years later (1885) he is still warmer in his defence, motivated by more extensive and recent reading of the poems in an edition that Coventry Patmore had lent him: 'I hold your [Bridges's] contemptuous opinion an unhappy mistake: he is a perfect artist and of a most spontaneous inspiration; it is as if Dorset life and Dorset landscape had taken flesh and tongue in the man ... he lacks fire; but who is perfect all round?' (LI 221). He manifests his esteem by composing music for two of Barnes's poems (229). It is especially indicative for his ideas on language that he expresses admiration for the spirit of Barnes's prose treatise on early English grammar. Though Hopkins qualifies his praise of Barnes's writings on linguistics, such as this one, he agrees with his concept of the native strength of the early language. Barnes saw the language of his Dorset neighbours as superior to the standard dialect because closer to

Old English, notably in the use of monosyllables and compounds. Hopkins cites *Went Hwome* as a 'fine and remarkable instance' of 'local colour' (LI 236). I quote the first stanza of three:

Upon the slope, the hedge did bound
The vield wi' blossom-whited zide,
An' charlock patches, yellow-dyed,
Did reach along the white-soil'd ground;
And vo'k a-comen up vrom meäd,
    Brought gil-cup meal upon the shoe;
Or went on where the road did leäd,
    Wi' smeechy doust vrom heel to toe,
As noon did smite, wi' burnen light,
The road so white, to Meldonley.

Hopkins finds that both the strong consonantal rhythm of the native substantives and the concise participial forms, rather than the suggestive novelty of the dialectal forms, impart poetic worth to Barnes's verse.

The discussion of dialect poetry shows that for Hopkins the poetical, the 'soul of poetry,' is not found in localisms per se. Despite the substantial virtues of Burns's dialect verse and Barnes's lack of energy or 'fire,' in his own restricted terms Hopkins declares the latter's poems in dialect to be the more 'poetical': in Barnes's work 'there is more true poetry than in Burns; I do not say of course vigour or passion or humour or a lot of things, but the soul of poetry, which I believe few Scotchmen have got' (LI 162).

Hopkins elsewhere indicates that the poetical is to be distinguished from dramatic energy, or philosophical depth, or rhetorical force. Writing to Dixon in 1886, he distinguishes the poetical from the philosophical. He cites Wordsworth as having a 'particular grace' of 'spiritual insight into nature,' which people 'perhaps think is above all the poet's gift.' He avers, to the contrary, that spiritual insight 'seems rather the philosopher's than the poet's.' At the same time, he grants that alongside the 'divine philosophy,' Wordsworth also had 'a lovely gift of verse.' In his ensuing discussion, he makes a further significant distinction between the poetical and the rhetorical. He finds in Wordsworth the major fault that afflicts all of English poetry: 'In his work there is ... *beaucoup à redire*: it is due to the universal fault of our literature, its weakness is rhetoric. The strictly poetical insight and inspiration of our poetry seems to me to be of the very finest, finer perhaps than the

Greek; but its rhetoric is inadequate ... By rhetoric I mean all the common and teachable element in literature, what grammar is to speech, what thoroughbass is to music, what theatrical experience gives to playwrights.' The design of *The Excursion* is not careful, so that it has much 'of dulness, superfluity, aimlessness, poverty of plan.' He also faults the structure of Wordsworth's sonnets, wondering why Wordsworth did 'not learn, or someone tell him that sonnets have a natural *charpente* never, or at least seldom broken through? For want of knowing this his inspired sonnets ... suffer from "hernia," and combine the tiro's blunder with the master's perfection' (LII 141–2).

Most concede that Wordworth's longer works, especially *The Excursion*, often lack structural discipline, but Hopkins's strictures about the composition of sonnets seem to arise from his own peculiar attachment to a rigid 4-4-3-3 structure that, while producing wonderful sonnets, for English verse is surely eccentric. The merits of his judgment of Wordsworth's sonnets, however, is not the point to be made here: it is that for Hopkins *rhetorical* form, though important for a text, is not an integral aspect of poeticalness. He further makes explicit the contrast of the poetical with the rhetorical in a key statement to Bridges about the proper reading of his oversized sonnet, *Spelt from Sibyl's Leaves*: 'Of this long sonnet above all remember what applies to all my verse, that it is ... made for performance and that its performance is not reading with the eye but loud, leisurely, *poetical* (not *rhetorical*) recitation, with long rests, long dwells on the rhyme and other marked syllables, and so on. This sonnet shd. be almost sung: it is most carefully timed in *tempo rubato*' (LI 246; my emphasis). Again, in his important late letter to Everard, he classes 'Macaulay's Lays [and] Aytoun's ditto' as 'rhetoric in verse,' 'very good of its rhetorical kind' but not 'genuine poetry' (LIV 219).

Hopkins further describes what he means by a 'poetical' reading in his 'Note on the Rhythm in "*The Wreck of the Deutschland*,"' where he advises the reader not to disguise 'the rhythm and rhyme, as some readers do, who treat poetry as if it were prose fantastically written to rule (which they mistakenly think the perfection of reading), but laying on the beats too much stress rather than too little' (P 118). In delivering his poem, he adds, the reader should pay particular attention to the metrical structure, notably to the foot and stanza divisions. The concluding sentence emphasizes that Hopkins by no means is suggesting that a reading neglect either verbal sense or the emotion attached to the sense: 'And so throughout let the stress be made to fetch out both the strength of the syllables and the meaning and feeling of the words' (P 118). The stress is in the service of the linguistic sense and the emotion proper to it, as well as of the music.

The poet subordinates aspects of verse that are often treated as the most important: energy or 'fire' (which Barnes lacks), philosophical charisma (which Wordsworth epitomizes), and rhetorical integrity (which classical poetry possesses but the English tradition is deficient in). In Hopkins's scheme the 'poetical' essence is not found in these features. Like local dialect, these features do not manifest the inscapes of speech, which, as the poet has told us, the artful repetitions of verse can make evident but do not embody. Thus, masters of verse, such as Tennyson and Swinburne and even Burns, despite his colourful dialect uses, do not succeed in presenting the 'current language,' which is to say the 'native and natural *rhythm* of speech' (LI 89; my emphasis). In poetry, the natural language may be 'to any degree heightened' by art, but the native speech rhythm is essential to its effectiveness. What constitutes this speech rhythm for Hopkins is elusive but in the end not completely enigmatic. Comparison of poets that he thinks succeed in presenting the rhythm and those that fail are indicative: Shakespeare, Milton, Barnes, Herrick, Herbert, Wordsworth, and evidently Whitman succeed. More specifically, the rhythms of Barnes, Herrick, and Herbert share, with the odour of certain flowers, the sights of regional landscapes, and the melodies of traditional songs, the power to evoke 'Westcountry instress.'

Hopkins makes negative judgments on the verse of Tennyson, Swinburne, and Burns, which may stem from the very virtuosity of their techniques that override and efface the currency of their language and native speech rhythms. To clarify what I suggest is Hopkins's point, we might take two small examples more or less at random. From Burns the opening of the well-known *Address to the Unco Guid*:

> O ye wha are sae guid yoursel',
>   Sae pious and sae holy,
> Ye've nought to do but mark and tell
>   Your neibors' fauts and folly!

'Pious and ... holy,' 'mark and tell,' 'fauts and folly': the problem Hopkins might find here, rather than the tautology of the pairs, may have to do with excessive ease in Burns's rhythm, making it too much art and too little speech.

We might compare lines from the first stanza of Barnes's *Went Hwome*, quoted above, which Hopkins commends:

Upon the slope, the hedge did bound
The vield wi' blossom-whited zide,
An' charlock patches, yellow-dyed,
Did reach along the white-soil'd ground.

One can justly see the stanza as 'homely.' Nevertheless, the series of compounds is striking: 'blossom-whited,' 'yellow-dyed,' 'white-soil'd.' While the compounds are not common adjectives of natural speech, the strong speech beat of each inconspicuously and effectively fits into the iambs of the verse, supporting while reconciling the tension between speech and verse. To test such a judgment, it might be interesting to listen behind Frost's closed door to oral delivery of the two poems. Which evokes more clearly current language?

For Hopkins, verse entails 'figures of spoken sound' that are repeated, the repetitions facilitating detachment of the speech inscape. A prime problem for the writer in Hopkins's conception of poetry is that in common or 'running' verse rhythm, the rhythmic repetitions of the foot patterns always threaten to reduce the naturalness – speechlikeness – of poetic expression. Hopkins's strictures may indicate that this is the case with Tennyson's and Burns's verse. Sprung rhythm avoids such perils by reconciling the apparently 'incompatible excellences' of irregular speech rhythm and regular verse rhythm. The other English writers that Hopkins finds to be successful as poets, we might infer, also manage such reconciliation through distinctive variations of regular rhythms, generally iambic, which he identifies as 'near the language of common talk' in both Greek and English (J 274), that make the rhythmic regularities less overt: Shakespeare's dramatic variations, Wordsworth's meditative progress, Herbert's subtle changes of pace, Milton's 'singular' cadences (LI 156). Even more speech-like, we may think, though at a cost to revelatory repetition, is Whitman's 'rugged' prose-poetry.

Throughout the nineteenth century it was generally accepted that language in the first place is speech, with writing providing a way of recording speech. Such an attitude is implicit in Hopkins's theories and in those of most linguistic specialists of his time. But Saussure's concept allows no place for speech sound in *langue*. As Genette states in quoting him, 'it is "impossible that sound, as a material element, should in itself be part of language [*langue*]."' Sound is simply something ancillary, a material that language uses (330).

Hopkins obviously recognized the symbolic aspect of language sound, the arbitrary matching of phonetic sequences to lexical sense, but he felt strongly that the properly linguistic meanings went beyond this. In his formulation, language is replete with affective human values that reside in the speech articulation. Graphic registration may communicate rhetorical mastery, philosophical profundity, even linguistic 'fire'; these, finally, are not dependent on vocal presentation. What is not communicated is the sensory charge of the verbal sound that underlies the meaning of *langue*. In an early note on Greek philosophy Hopkins distinguishes the universal and concrete moments of the 'Idea' and the 'name' (i.e., the word sound) by adducing an image of a hand and glove: 'Taking the Idea for a hand and the name for the glove left behind, then although to handle it by the concrete may leave it a dry crumpled piece of skin, abstraction may as injuriously blow it out into a graceless bladdery animation' (quoted in Brown 159–60). The 'Idea' alone, produced negatively by sound contrasts, is 'a graceless bladdery animation,' the unfilled glove is the physical sound without meaning, a 'dry crumpled piece of skin.' The whole hand and glove, the complete verbal form, lives in the concretion of verbal articulation.

In including a proper poetical component, Hopkins's concept of language meaning goes beyond grammatical relations and the lexical and logical meanings of plain expository prose, or even of artful rhetorical prose or mnemonic verse. 'Thirty days hath September,' he says, is like prose in its focus on plain lexical meanings. Despite its verse form, it is not poetry. 'But if [verse] has a meaning and *is meant to be heard for its own sake* it will be poetry' (J 289; my emphasis). Poetry is not concerned in the first place with informing; as poetry it appeals to human responsiveness by means of the sensory content of the speech figures.

Stress and intonation are among the primary linguistic instruments of making such appeal. The affective element in poetical language will sometimes cause alterations in normal prose inflection, as Hopkins asserts in the lecture notes for 'Rhythm and Other Structural Parts of Rhetoric – Verse.' 'Emotional emphasis,' he states, 'will sometimes light up notes on unemphatic syllables and not follow the verbal stresses and pitches' (J 270). I have already referred to Dwight Bolinger's statement that intonation responds more directly to feeling than other aspects (202). Bolinger has further generalized, with particular reference to present-day linguistics, that 'the overintellectualization of speech by casting all of its manifestations in the mold of syntactic and morphological abstraction has obscured the true nature of intonation' (viii). Hopkins's conception, well illustrated in his poetry, would carry Bolinger's idea beyond stress and intonation to include most aspects of linguistic sound. For the poet, it seems that, in addition to intonation and stress, all the indefinable positive values of the segmental phones, of their collocations and concatenations, have systematic significances replete with human feeling.

In Hopkins's conception the poetical component inheres in figures of speech sound, and the prime content of the figures is the inscape of the complex sense experience and especially of the feelings and emotions attached to it. The figures are naturally iconic, their effects, like feelings, unanalysable in logical terms. In his mature lyrics Hopkins's narrator often represents himself as caught in a Wordsworthian 'spontaneous overflow of powerful feeling,' and he conveys much of the emotion directly through the icons of the sounds. The role of feeling in language sound is especially obvious in the poet's frequent use of exclamatory language in his own verse: the breathless 'O my chevalier!' and 'ah my dear!' in *The Windhover*, or the opening cry of the sonnet, *The Starlight Night*, in which exclamation points mark each of the first eleven lines.

> Look at the stars! look, look up at the skies!
> O look at all the fire-folk sitting in the air!

In similar fashion, rhetorical questions and prayerful invocations also often animate his verse, as in the tortured emotional questioning in *Carrion Comfort* (the italics indicate non-metrical 'outrides'):

> But ah, but O thou ter*rible*, why wouldst thou rude on me
> Thy wring-world right foot rock? Lay a lionlimb against me? Scan
> With darksome devouring eyes my bruised bones? And fan,
> O in turns of tem*pest*, me heaped *there*; me frantic to avoïd thee and flee?
>
> (5–8)

The poet characteristically focuses on his emotional reaction to the objects of his representations, aiming through the soundscape to lead to the sensory inner form – to an instress of the human feeling in the word sounds. If 'O!' and 'ah!' are standard symbolic English lexical items carrying conventional meanings, at the same time, in an oral reading, where Hopkins believes that the poetic element is to be found, they also have the iconic force of spontaneous expressions of feeling.

Also carrying iconic significance in the linguistic continuum are some of Hopkins's surprising stress markings. The emotional component often leads the poet to depart from usual word stress, as numerous of his stress markings in the verse manuscripts show. His placing of the stresses for line 3 of *The Windhover*, for example, '[ríding] / Of the rólling level únderneath him steady áir, and stríding /,' indicates a substantial deviation from ordinary delivery in assigning two stresses to the preposition 'únderneath,' with no stresses on the surrounding lexically prominent adjectives 'level' and 'steady.' Elizabeth Schneider finds Hopkins mistaking his own principles in such markings (85–93), but the non-standard linguistic emphasis may be seen as central in expressing the poet's wonder at the 'mastery' of the bird in flight. We might compare the emotional flatness of a putative line in trochaic metre that places standard stress on the adjectives: '[ríding] / the rólling lével stéady áir underneath him/.' The poet's marking directs that the imperatives of the affective content should take precedence over the usual sentence stressing. Instead of stress being a transparent vehicle for emotively neutral conveyance of linguistic meaning, here it acts as an opaque icon, immediately expressive of the pertinent emotion, in this case, awe. I discuss Schneider's contrary analysis in the next chapter.

The studied complexity of the sound patterns in Hopkins's verse confirms that in his conception of verse, not only the stress and intonation, but *all* of the complex sound patterns of his verse, involving metre, alliteration, vowel gradation, consonant juxtaposition, and so on, are designed to convey the inscape of poetical feeling iconically – not by logical symbols, but directly through the sense of sound – and furthermore that for Hopkins such feeling is a major component of its poetical inscape. Bernard O'Donoghue makes a related claim for Seamus Heaney's poetry, emphasizing throughout his book on the poet's language that 'Heaney's allying of "phonetics and feeling" is of great importance for the interpretation of his language' (80). Such an alliance involves one of Heaney's major debts to Hopkins.

Poetry, says Hopkins, 'is in fact speech only employed to carry the inscape of speech for the inscape's sake.' 'Figures' of speech sound convey the emotional inscape. Hopkins does not conceive the figures appropriate to poetry as being embedded in particular grammatical, syntactic, or colloquial structures. Though it may happen that the repetitions involve such structures, that fact is secondary. His theory is predicated on fundamentally phonic sequences. The imitable merit that he finds in the Anglo-Saxon resides in its heavily consonantal, predominantly substantive monosyllables and in the syllabic strength of its typically Germanic compounding. These features of the lexical sound in his verse impart to it, in his terms, a 'native' character:

Glory be to God for dappled things –
   For skies of couple-colour as a brinded cow;
     For rose-moles all in stipple upon trout that swim;
Fresh-firecoal chestnut-falls; finches' wings;
   Landscape plotted and pieced – fold, fallow, and plough;
     And all trades, their gear and tackle and trim.   *Pied Beauty* 1–6

The collocations of the segmental sounds – the consonants and vowels of 'dappled things,' 'brinded cow,' 'rose-moles,' 'trout that swim,' and so on – make effective speech figures, which are found in the intrinsic character of the phonetic sequences. The repetitions of the metrical patterns and of the rhyme and alliteration, which 'often' and 'after' the inscape, facilitate detachment of the speech figure 'to the mind.' The poetical value of the figure lies in the inscape of the feeling attached to the figure, feeling broadly conceived to comprehend both direct sensory and emotional content.

The poetical significance of the speech figure – of the inscape of the speech sound – is 'over and above meaning, at least the grammatical, historical, and logical meaning' (J 289). The poet's art conforms the verse patterns to the speech figures. The genius of sprung rhythm, its advantage over what the poet calls 'running rhythm,' is its naturalness as 'the rhythm of common speech and of written prose.' At the same time, as Hopkins's practice and commentary on other poets makes clear, any common verse pattern *can* fulfil the end of 'oftening' the inscape of speech sound. The fact that *God's Grandeur* and *Starlight Night* are composed in 'standard rhythm' (P 361, 363) does not abridge the possible effectiveness of the poems any more than it limits Shakespeare's or Milton's blank verse. Nevertheless, sprung rhythm, exemplified by Hopkins's own *Deutschland* and by Milton's choruses in *Samson Agonistes* (see LI 45; LII 15), has the marked advantage of natural propinquity to speech rhythm in revealing the poetical quality.

While Hopkins is one among many who have attributed special meaning to poetry, he is among very few prominent writers who have theorized in any depth about the nature of such meaning. His ideas on the subject are diffused in various writings and remain in some respects incomplete; at the same time, they are a product of extended study and thought over much of his life. Most signally, as we have seen in this chapter, Hopkins maintains that poetry is speech, which requires utterance for its value to be realized, and he indicates that versification is normally, but not always, required to effect a framing of speech sound inscape and to facilitate its detachment of it for contemplation.

Hopkins's idea of poetic language as speech agrees with assumptions that were common well into the twentieth century, while it stands in opposition to the linguistic theory that has since become dominant, by which linguistic sound has only negative value, and metre and rhyme and other devices of poetry constitute a 'secondary modelling system' that is not part of language proper. On the contrary, like the Prague theorists, Hopkins sees the poetical as one aspect of language meaning itself. His ideas were nurtured especially by his deep experience with classical learning and study of Greek and Latin poetry that began with and foregrounded metrics, that is, with sound pattern. In that spirit, he approached his discussions and creation of poetry; and his highly theoretical predisposition developed the original concept of poetic meaning – poeticalness – that this chapter has largely explored. It has centred on sprung rhythm's aptness to realize his idea of that meaning by conforming the regular rhythmic repetitions of poetry to the speech rhythms of 'natural' language, specifically to those of 'native,' characteristically English speech.

Hopkins finds in the music of speech, then, the essence of the poetical, a kind of linguistic significance beyond that which grammar and logic determine. At the same time, his idea of poeticalness goes beyond the traditional assumption that specifically poetic significance, while undoubtedly positive, is transcendent and ineffable. In the view of critics such as George Steiner and Allen Tate, following Coleridge in *Definitions of Poetry*, the concerns of art and science are at opposite poles. Tate baldly states, 'Poetry is not only quite different from science but in its essence is opposed to science' (Brown 200). Hopkins would hardly have accepted the opposition. Highly inquisitive and living in a century of epochal scientific discoveries, when understanding the great discoveries being made was by and large still possible for the educated person, he was much concerned with the accomplishments of science. For him its materials were also materials for poetry (187–207). More integrally, he found the essence of poetic meaning in the physical phenomenon of speech sound. He celebrated the physicality of sound in his poetry, his theory, and his commentary. In his conception art's presentation of the physical 'scapes' can lead to revelation of inner form, the inscape, just as science's exploration of the scapes of the phenomenal world can conduce to, if not manifest, such revelation.

In Hopkins's terms, a scape is an outer form; informing it is the inscape, closely but not directly related to the outer form. The earthly scape that poetry deals with is that of human speech sound; its particular interest is in penetrating to – instressing – the inscape of the speech figure. The commonest way poetry uses to lead the reader to this inscape is through repetition of the speech figures, with the aim of 'detaching' the figure for contemplation. Underlying such ideas and at the heart of his thought is Hopkins's realist metaphysics. His development as a philosophical thinker began and matured with his avid study of Greek idealism at Oxford. From the outset he rejected positivism and materialism, but at the same time he retained his fascination with the phenomenal world, and in his late twenties he found in the realism of John Duns Scotus a thoroughly congenial system of thinking that incorporated both ideal and material.

Since Hopkins's neologisms *instress* and *inscape* are central to his metaphysics and to his poetics of sound, in chapter 4 this study explores insofar as possible the meanings and implications of these words. His studies and notes on Greek philosophy and his adoption of Scotus's version of realism are especially crucial for the subject. Prior to that more thorough investigation, however, it will be useful to treat less speculative, more practical aspects of his poetic theory and art, which may at the same time bring us closer to his metaphysical speculations. The intervening two chapters treat problems that are less vexed and more directly relevant to Hopkins's poetic craft. Chapter 2 takes up the second aspect of sprung rhythm, its accommodation of verse music, and chapter 3 deals with what Hopkins aptly labels 'lettering,' the repetitions of various kinds of letter sounds in end-rhyme, alliteration, assonance, and complex orchestrations of sounds such as those particularly characteristic of Welsh and Scandinavian versification.

2 Sprung Rhythm: The Music of Verse

In 'Poetry and Verse' Hopkins indicates that human speech embodies the pre-eminent values of language that are realized in poetry. He states that native speech rhythms embody most markedly the 'inscape' of speech, whose revelation is the object of poetry, and he implies in a letter to his brother Everard that prose as well as verse can qualify as poetry, prose conceivably being more beautiful than verse, 'even though debarred of [verse's] symmetrical beauties' (LIV 220). Such statements seem to subordinate the role of versification. Notwithstanding, as the complexity of Hopkins's own verse testifies, versification has intrinsic *poetic* significance for him, and its nature and techniques are a major preoccupation. He theorizes about it repeatedly, not only in his lecture notes, entitled in manuscript 'Rhythm and Other Structural Parts of Rhetoric – Verse' (J 267–88), but also in extensive analyses and commentary found throughout his correspondence with his poet-friends, who looked to him as an authoritative theoretician of verse art.

Despite his granting primacy to speech rhythm in 'Poetry and Verse,' in statements made elsewhere – for instance, when clarifying his reasons for employing sprung rhythm – Hopkins virtually assigns equal importance to the rhythmic structure of verse. While asserting that sprung rhythm by nature is 'logaoedic' (P 115–16) and describing it to Bridges as 'nearest to the rhythm of prose, that is the native and natural rhythm of speech,' he represents it as reconciling speech with the strong cadence of verse, with both speech and verse rhythm remaining important: 'Why do I employ sprung rhythm at all?' he asks rhetorically, responding, because it combines '*opposite*, and one wd. have thought, incompatible *excellences*, markedness of rhythm ... and naturalness of expression' (LI 46; my emphases). In sprung rhythm, then, two kinds of verbal music merge: the *music of speech*, with its natural recurrence of stress, and the *music of verse* with its regular stress repetition.

In 'Poetry and Verse,' the poet draws a clear distinction between the use of verse form and the nature of poetry, and he does not rely on specifying subject matter – contrasting poetic with prosaic – to distinguish poeticalness. His stance of valorizing speech rhythm allows that the free verse nascent in the practice of the time, or prose of a certain artistry, such as the English versions of the Psalms, can embody the poetical quality. At the same time, his own powerful verse structures strongly imply, and his correspondence substantiates, that for him the repeating structures of verse can have their own proper poetic value by virtue of their regular embodiment of natural speech rhythm.

Also indicating that the regularity of verse music may play a major role in poeticalness is Hopkins's postulation that the units of pitched music, themselves characteristically regular, are like those of verse in being a 'recasting' of speech: Verse is 'the recasting of speech into sound-words, sound-clauses and sound-sentences of uniform commensurable length and accentuations'; pitched music likewise is 'the recasting of speech used in a wide sense, of vocal utterance,' into 'uniform' measures in which 'the musical syllable is the note, the musical foot or word the bar, the bars in double time stand for double feet, etc.' (J 273). He also associates verse with music in the 'Preface on Rhythm' prefixed to *The Wreck of the Deutschland*, declaring that sprung rhythm is 'the rhythm of all but the most monotonously regular music, so that in the words of choruses and refrains and in songs written closely to music it arises' (P 117). The association suggests that verse structure partakes of the aesthetic qualities inherent in musical structure.

The features that sprung rhythm reconciles, speech rhythm and verse rhythm, evoke two venerable concepts of poetry. On the one hand, rhythmic naturalness agrees with Aristotle's theory of mimesis, except that the rhythm's imitation is not of an 'action,' as Aristotle prescribes, but of natural speech patterns. On the other hand, markedness of rhythm is a property of verse that agrees with the ancient assumption of *ars musica* that both poetry and pitched music are primarily organized sound. St Augustine in his *De Musica*, which is devoted chiefly to verse, defines music as 'ars bene modulandi' / 'the art of measuring sound well'; it is by virtue of rhythm and metre that poetry may be classed as music. An assumption of this theory, as O.B. Hardison Jr asserts, is that the repeating sounds of poetry are 'constitutive' of special significance whose 'power comes to it through music' (22).

The notion of a mimesis based on speech sound is compatible with treatises of classical rhetoric. The Ciceronian *Rhetorica ad Herennium,* treats rhetorical *construction* as a process that 'makes all parts of a composition equally elegant' (Hardison 22). By virtue of its simulation of prose cadence, Hopkins asserts, sprung rhythm is naturally rhetorical: 'it is the nearest to the rhythm of prose, that is the native and natural rhythm of speech, the most rhetorical and emphatic of all possible rhythms' (LI 46). His distancing of poetry from rhetoric elsewhere appears to contradict such a statement, but in his formulation sprung rhythm is only proselike and rhetorical by virtue of embodying the *sound* figures of speech. The repeating *verse* figures themselves are not tied to word meanings, but rather can recur in completely different contexts of lexical sense: 'Verse is speech having a marked figure, order/ of sounds *independent of meaning* and such as can be shifted from one word or words to others without changing. It is figure of spoken sound' (LI 246; my emphasis). The rhetorical *sound pattern* of verse, then, conforms to the poetical speech figure and the intended poetical effect rather than to the logical meaning.

Stress for Hopkins is the crucial factor in sprung rhythm's successful melding of speech and verse; it both segments the verse units and simulates speech cadences. He states baldly to Bridges that 'stress is the life of [sprung rhythm]' (LI 52); to Dixon that its 'stress [is] more *of* a stress' (LII 39); and to Everard most fully: 'As poetry is emphatically speech, speech purged of dross like gold in the furnace, so it must have emphatically the essential elements of speech. Now emphasis itself ... is one of these: sprung rhythm makes verse stressy; it purges it to an emphasis as much brighter, livelier, more lustrous than the regular but commonplace emphasis of common rhythm as poetry in general is brighter than common speech. But, this it does by a return from that regular emphasis towards, not up to the more picturesque irregular emphasis of talk – without however becoming itself lawlessly irregular; then it would not be art' (LIV 218–19). In this important late letter (1885), he underscores his view of poetry as having its true existence in its oral presentation, with stress being the primary aspect of its heard sounds. Silent reading gives one a chance to study it, but only to the end of understanding its performance in speech.

All poetry is speech, but not vice versa. Hopkins is emphatic in distinguishing speech presented as poetry from rhetorical speech. In his 'Preface on Rhythm,' which introduces *Deutschland*, he instructs the reader 'strongly to mark the beats of the measure ... not disguising the rhythm and the rhyme, as some readers do, who treat poetry as if it were prose fantastically written to rule (which they mistakenly think the perfection of reading), but laying on the beat too much stress rather than too little' (P 118). And more explicitly distinguishing poetical from rhetorical effect, he accompanies a text of *Spelt from Sybil's Leaves* that he sends to Bridges with instructions to remember 'what applies to all my verse, that it is, as living art should be, made for performance and that its performance is not reading for the eye but loud, leisurely, *poetical* (not *rhetorical*) recitation, with long rests, long dwells on the rhyme and other marked syllables, and so on' (LI 245; my emphases).

Stress is the 'life' of sprung rhythm, equally important for enforcing verse regularity and for simulating speech naturalness. In his lecture notes on verse rhythm, Hopkins defines stress as a kind of accent: 'emphatic accent.' He contrasts 'accent of stress' with 'accent of pitch': 'We may think of words as heavy bodies ... Now every visible palpable body has a centre of gravity round which it is in balance and a centre of illumination ... up to which it is lighted and down from which it is shaded. The centre of gravity is like the accent of stress, the highspot like the accent of pitch, for pitch is like light and colour, stress like weight.' He grasps quite well the linguistic complexities of stress and intonation in English: 'the accent of stress [is] strong, that of pitch weak – only they go together for the most part' (J 268–9). Every word 'has its emphatic accent ... which being changed the word becomes meaningless ... or changes meaning ... But besides the stress or emphasis and pitch or intonation of single syllables one against another there is stress or emphasis and pitch or intonation running through the sentence and setting word against word as stronger or as higher pitched' (J 270). Hopkins is recognizing that what he calls the accents of pitch and stress often have phonological value for the meanings of separate words and of syntactic structure, and recognizing that both sentences and individual words have stress and intonation patterns. Tellingly for his poetic practice and concept of verse, however, Hopkins adds, 'But *emotional intonation*, especially when not closely bound to the particular words will sometimes light up notes on unemphatic syllables and not follow the verbal stress and pitches' (271; my emphasis). In other words, emotional emphasis can sometimes alter usual *sentence* intonation, and also the sentence stress.

The meanings produced by what the poet labels 'emotional intonation' are not derived from the 'logical' sense. In semiotic terms, the 'emotional' is iconic, while the 'logical' is symbolic. In the symbol, there is an arbitrary two-sided relationship between sign and signified, while in the icon, sign and signified almost merge. For the two kinds of emphasis, Hopkins proffers the example of French, by which 'the accent of stress ... receives any special or sentence emphasis (*logical emphasis*) which is to be given, the tonic accent ... receives diffused *emotional emphasis*' (J 270; my emphasis). By this conception, emotional emphasis – which is particularly proper to the strong affective values of poetry – can alter intonation pattern, and it can pull the sentence stress pattern with it. Failure to recognize the emotional, expressive role of poetic emphasis leads Elizabeth Schneider astray in her analyses of Hopkins's stress markings. She states that the poet breaks his own 'unbreakable law' that in sprung rhythm 'sense stress always determines metrical stress' (89). Many of the markings, she claims, are 'unjustified in terms either of rhythm ... or any imaginable meaning, however subtle' (85–6), and she proposes numerous examples of his mis-stressing, for instance, his stress markings of the last line of *The Lantern out of Doors*: '*Théir* ransom, *théir* rescue, *ánd* first, fást, last fríend' (89–90). Schneider is following Father Walter Ong's influential claim that sprung rhythm 'does not merely utilize sense stresses; it grows out of them, is constituted by them alone' (112). But Ong's understanding of the poet's several statements about the naturalness of his rhythm, that it is 'the rhythm of common speech and written prose,' fails to recognize that the stress and intonation patterns are not tied fast to the ordinary logical sense, but can be altered by emotional significance. Allowing for this, the stresses indicated by Hopkins – a poet with a sensitive ear conditioned by extensive experience with music and scrupulous in his punctuation and use of diacritics – are quite performable, though at times certainly unusual.

The linguist Paul Kiparsky declares correctly that 'there is no such law' as Schneider propounds – that is, that for Hopkins 'the sense stress always determines the metrical stress' (Schneider 89). But Kiparsky also misinterprets; he states that the poet's description of stress 'cannot mean that sprung rhythm lines have a fixed number of actual phonological stresses,' since Hopkins is talking not about ordinary language use but about metrics (307). Quoting from the explanations of sprung rhythm in the Preface and a letter to Dixon, Kiparsky claims 'It is clear that "accent," "stress," and "slack syllables" are meant to refer not to accent in the phonological sense but to strong and weak METRICAL POSITIONS' (307; his capitals). Kiparsky, then, sets up a distinction between *actual* stress and *metrical* stress.

Though his essay is particularly valuable for its analysis of metrical quantity, Kiparsky is also mistaken about the poet's stress markings. On the one hand, Schneider thinks they are not performable, but they demonstrably are. On the other hand, Kiparsky thinks that they are not applicable to 'actual' stress, but rather are intended as indicators of metrical stress, controlled by quantity, not of contrastive stress signifying language meaning. However, Hopkins continually insists that his poems are oral artefacts, and that the stresses of sprung rhythm are 'actual.' The verse depends on bringing out the stresses. 'Poetry is emphatically speech' (LIV 218). Verse needs to be read with 'stress and declaim' (LI 52). It should not be read 'as if it were prose fantastically written to rule ... but laying on the beats too much stress rather than too little' (P 118).

Kiparsky and Schneider do not take into account that in Hopkins's verse 'emotional emphasis' often affects and supersedes what appears to be linguistically natural, what Ong terms 'sense stress.' Ong likewise does not allow that the 'sense,' especially in poetry, also includes affective factors. For Hopkins, the 'emotional emphasis' of poetry is mainly systematic. It does not vary according to the performers' judgment, but is an affective aspect of the language system that the poet is applying. To supply a desired systematic 'spelling' that would assimilate the emotional content of a poem into the graphic system, the poet uses a set of diacritics, especially for his sprung-rhythm works. His stress indicators mark 'actual stress' which is both metrical and sense stress, part of linguistic meaning broadly understood to include feeling. Such a concept of stress fits in with Roman Jakobson's linguistic scheme, which makes a place for 'emotive' or 'expressive' language meaning, typified by the lyric first person that focuses on the speaker (1987, esp. 66–7, 70).

Kiparsky asserts that Hopkins 'uses the word "stress" both for the metrical beat and for phonological accent, distinguishing between "stresses of sense," that is, phonological accent, and "metrical stresses" (or "stresses of the verse")' (307), but he does not analyse the poet's applications of the distinction, which are few and scattered and always made to verse in common rhythm. Hopkins does not at all apply the distinction to his sprung-rhythm verse, which indeed, as he states, *cannot be counterpointed* (P 116; my emphasis). A division of metrical stress from sense stress predicates counterpoint. In his lecture notes on metrics, he observes that in Greek verse 'the scanning is by time and rhythmic beat, that is beat belonging only to the rhythm-words, not to the sense words' (J 279). Hopkins thus is transferring to vernacular verse a distinction originating in classical metrics, and he does this for his own work in his notes and markings for only two poems: *Tom's Garland*, whose rhythm he explicitly specifies in manuscript as '*not* sprung' (P 484–5; my emphasis) or as 'common rhythm' (P 485), and *Ashboughs,* which in manuscript directly follows *Tom's Garland* and clearly is in the same standard rhythm. The two works, then, do not belong in Kiparsky's listing of sprung rhythm works (Kiparsky 389).

A note by the poet describes the unusual diacritics of *Tom's Garland*: 'Heavy stresses marked double, thus, ˝ and *stresses of sense,* independent of the *natural stress of the verse,* thus, ``' (P 485; my emphases). The distinction that applies here accords with the poet's description of coun-terpoint of standard rhythm, by which 'each line has two different coexisting scansions.' Hopkins says that the counterpoint essentially mounts 'stress of sense' on the established stress pattern, and the reader feels both stresses. If the poet persists in the counterpointing, however, the 'secondary or "mounted rhythm,"' which becomes 'necessarily a sprung rhythm, overpowers the original or conventional one and then this becomes superfluous and may be got rid of; by taking that last step you reach simple sprung rhythm' (LII 15). The sprung rhythm is 'simple' because it has reconciled the 'sense' stress wholly with the metrical stress, making the two coincide at all points. Counterpoint is no longer possible.

There are four points in the text of *Tom's Garland* (lines 2, 4, 5, 17 twice) at which the poet's marks indicate that the 'stresses of sense' vary from the 'stresses of the verse.' The only other poem in which Hopkins uses the double grave (``) to mark counterpoint is *Ashboughs* (lines 2, 3, 5, 6), evidently composed at the same late time (September 1887) as *Tom's Garland.* He distinguishes between stresses of 'sense' and 'metrics' once more in a letter to Bridges in 1880 in analysing an iambic verse of Wyatt. He places three small circles under stressed syllables, two circles filled in, one not: 'the black ball marking the real or heard stress, the white the dumb or conventional one' (LI 109). The small white and black circles occur again without commentary in his textual marking of one version of *Tom's Garland* (MS II, pl. 492).

Harry Ploughman, written at the same time as *Ashboughs* and *Tom's Garland,* professedly *is* in sprung rhythm (P 480), and its metrical mark-ings accordingly differ in important respects from the other two works. The marks for *Harry Ploughman* juxtapose stresses on adjacent syllables, thereby distinguishing monosyllabic feet. They indicate several 'out-rides' (a characteristic 'licence of sprung rhythm' [P 116–17]), and they do not use or need the double-grave 'sense stress' mark. His list of diacritical marks for the poem (MSII 48) accordingly includes no diacritic for sense stress.

Hopkins, then, consistently conceives of the stress of sprung rhythm as an 'actual' stress that is always realized in the reading. It often carries emotional emphasis through loudness, pitch, and/or duration, thereby conveying a properly linguistic meaning, an *iconic* significance above and beyond the usual symbolic sense signalled by arbitrary sound contrasts. At the same time, while Hopkins's markings of sprung rhythm stress can indicate displacement of more usual phrasal or sentence stressing, reconfiguring the stress and intonation patterns, he almost never alters word accent, which, as he explicitly recognizes, often would alter the word meaning (J 270; he instances '*présent*' and '*presént*'). As a result, his stressing seldom leaves in doubt the 'logical' sense of a sprung-rhythm sentence. The poet's addition of emotional significance through his marking generally enhances rather than interferes with the meaning. Thus, his markings of *Spelt from Sybil's Leaves*, which Schneider cites as examples of misplaced stress, if accepted as operative markers add substantially to the poetical significance: 'self ín self stéepèd and páshed – quíte' (line 5); 'thóughts agáinst thoughts ín groans grínd' (line 14). Though the stresses on the prepositions 'ín' and 'agáinst' replace usual contrastive stresses on 'self,' 'thoughts,' and 'groan,' the logical sense is clear, and the emotional content is phonetically augmented.

In his sprung-rhythm stressing Hopkins does not adhere to a word-class hierarchy like that which holds in Old English versification, to which Hopkins's sprung rhythm is sometimes compared. The Old English system accords stress to the more important lexical classes such as nouns, adjectives, and verbs, but Hopkins sometimes leaves these word classes unstressed in favour of prepositions, conjunctions, and pronouns: 'théir ransom, théir rescue,' 'self ín self,' 'agáinst thoughts.' The poet may vary phrasal stress (e.g., stressing 'ín' rather than either occurrence of 'self'), but his variations have phonetic limits. For one thing, as I have mentioned, he rarely stresses syllables contrary to word-stress; isolated exceptions are his stresses on the second syllable of 'shouldér' in *Harry Ploughman* (line 4) and – in one manuscript version – on the second syllable of 'liftéd' (line 14). Both of these stress marks follow even stronger marks on preceding syllables (´´, ^) and occur in 'burden-lines' that 'might be recited by a chorus' (P 480). Moreover, the poet acknowledges the experimental nature of the sprung rhythm of *Harry Ploughman*, warning Bridges that the text may strike him as 'intolerably violent and artificial' (481). His caution could be applied equally to the two poems in 'common rhythm' written at the same late time, *Ashboughs* and *Tom's Garland*, both having unusually complex metrics. Another limitation on his unusual emphases is his avoidance of stressing unclosed monosyllables that have short vowels ('a,' 'the').

Hopkins's stress markings show that his concept of language includes emotional iconic elements that can reconfigure the common prosodic patterns of language that contrastive phonology identifies. An interesting example occurs in *Windhover* (line 4), where performing the poet's stress marks causes the intonation contour to follow the stresses upwards twice on 'úndernéath' but to remain flat on 'level' and 'steady': 'the rólling level úndernéath him steady áir.' While the ordinary word stresses are unaffected, the common sentence stress is notably altered by emotional factors (the alteration reinforced by a mimesis of lexical sense in the unstressing of 'level' and 'steady'). Kiparsky's analysis of Hopkins's sprung rhythm, astute in elucidating the poet's conception of quantity, is vitiated by a failure to recognize the role of affective aspects of Hopkins's stress marking, leading him to misapply the poet's limited distinction between 'actual' and 'metrical' stress and also to cite examples in which the linguist alleges that Hopkins's text indicates either too few or too many 'actual' stresses. Thus, he says that, while in *Spring and Fall* Hopkins marks four stresses in the first line, there are 'two or perhaps three actual stresses, certainly not four.' While the poet marks the line with four stresses – 'Márgarét, áre you gríeving?' – Kiparsky's analysis identifies two or three: 'Márgaret, are [or áre'] you gríeving?' He asserts, on the other hand, that the line of *The Loss of the Eurydice*, which Hopkins marks 'Wept, wífe; wept, swéetheart wóuld be óne,' in actuality 'has more than four stesses' (presumably, 'Wépt, wífe; wépt swéetheart wóuld be óne,' line 106) (Kiparsky 307). Notwithstanding such claims, emotional emphasis clearly can add stress to the last syllable of 'Márgarét' and to 'áre,' and it can reduce stress on the two instances of 'wept.' While present-day phonologists mostly ignore emotional emphasis, thereby suggesting that it is a matter of idiosyncratic *parole*, for Hopkins it is part of the system: 'actual' stress is more than a matter of phonological contrast.

At the same time, Kiparsky's careful analysis of Hopkins's differentiations of metrical length bears out the poet's claim that he has carefully timed his sprung rhythm verse. One important intrinsic rule in Hopkins's verse that Kiparsky reveals is that all the syllables in 'split weak position' (i.e., when the 'slack' part of the foot consists of more than one syllable)

are quite short by nature (312–13). Aside from certain systematic exceptions, these syllables have short vowels not closed by consonant. Such
short syllables may be read 'flyingly,' to use the poet's term (P 118),
making the stressed syllable potentially equal in duration even to three
or more unstressed syllables. The timing is consistent with the analyses in
Hopkins's lecture notes on verse rhythm, where he cites the pronuncia-
tions of *véterinary* as '4 + 1 + 1 + 1 + 1' and *incómparable* as '1 + 4 + 1 + 1 + 1'
(J 271), suggesting how he might have elaborated the 'mathematics'
that, as he claims, guided his metrical composition (LIV 219). These
timings would suit a four-syllable slack, making the stressed syllable equal
to the whole of the slack. The timing of a brief or non-existent slack may
be extended either by lengthening the stressed syllables, by pauses, or by
'treading and dwelling' (P 118).

Stress *is* the 'life' of sprung rhythm: for its power to effect communication, it is the dominant natural feature of the 'music of speech,' and, for
its control of quantitative regularity, it is dominant in the 'music of
verse.' It is both the salient element in the 'picturesque irregular emphasis of talk,' which is speech music, and also that which marks the recurring foot divisions, the verse music that keeps the rhythm from 'becoming
lawlessly irregular' (LIV 219). As we have seen, Hopkins emphasizes the
importance of quantity for verse symmetry, and he states that in contrast
to Greek practice, English quantity consists of both *length* and *strength*.
The next chapter treats the poet's view of quantitative strength, which
he achieves in his own verse especially by means of the repetitions of
'lettering,' rhyming. The remainder of this chapter deals largely with the
ways that Hopkins works to achieve uniform length in the speech 'figures' of his verse, through syllable quantity, and line and stanza length. It
is mostly by virtue of quantitative length that verse may be called music
in St Augustine's sense of 'good measuring' and that it and pitched
music come together.

Along with his parents and siblings, Hopkins was a devotee of the most
prominent art forms and was familiar with the accepted authorities.
Ruskin's early influence helps to account for the fact that J.H. Parker's
A Glossary of Terms Used in ... Architecture became 'perhaps the most
lastingly influential book in his early education.' His admiration for
Ruskin also helps to explain his serious moves in later youth towards a
career as artist (White 21, 79–83). He read and composed poetry throughout most of his life, while a passion for music and for musical composition blossomed in his later years. As he confesses to Bridges in 1881,
when he was in the gloom of Liverpool, music came to seem his last

refuge: 'Every impulse and spring of art seems to have died in me, except for music' (LI 124). Although he never learned to play an instrument expertly and felt his lack of training in music theory, his experimentation in musical composition and his commentaries on music show his characteristic independence and theoretical originality (see J. Stevens; cf. Hollahan 160–2). His later verse especially reflects his ardent affection for music, which he displays in several well-known poems: in the musical subjects of *Henry Purcell*, *At the Wedding March*, *The Woodlark*, and the *The Leaden Echo and the Golden Echo*; the use of conventional musical notations (*rallentando, sforzando, staccato*) in the manuscript texts of *The Sea and the Skylark*, *Spring*, and *In the Valley of the Elwy* (see Feeney 20); and in his continual writings about and experimenting with rhythm in the later poems.

Rhythm was central for Hopkins. Speculating about the origin of rhythm, he imagines that 'Once music and verse were perhaps one but were differenced by dwelling on the mere pitch and lettering [word sounds] respectively' (J 268), guessing that they coincided in early classical Greece. He agrees, furthermore, with Frederick Gore Ouseley that musical time 'arose from dance music,' inclining to believe that 'verse-time arose from the dance too' (LI 119). The similar development of the medieval French rondeau and ballade from dance forms that scholars have noted lends warrant to such a supposition. As a theoretician of art, the great project of Hopkins's later life was a book on 'Dorian measure,' which would comprehend a treatment of 'rhythm in general' and was to bring out 'the most fundamental principles of art ... almost a philosophy of art' (LI 246–7). His description of the Dorian measure shows further the poet's ambition for the book; he calls it 'the true scansion of perhaps half or more of Greek and Latin lyric verse ... a great and unexpected discovery.' He asserts to Patmore that he 'can now set metre and music both of them on a scientific footing which will be final like the law of gravity' (LIII 367–77). To Bridges in the same late year of his life, 1887, he says he has 'written a great deal' of the book (LI 254, 256). But these indications and other sketchy explanations in his correspondence (e.g., LI 233–5) are all that remain to indicate the direction of his thinking. Even allowing for the poet's hyperbole, in the light of his originality and learning the disappearance of his broad conjectures on rhythm is certainly unfortunate.

Hopkins particularly shows his view of verse and music as sister arts in his Preface on sprung rhythm. He describes 'verse counterpoint' as 'something answerable to counterpoint in music'; the 'rests' of sprung rhythm as being like those 'in music'; the rhythm itself as 'the rhythm of all but the most monotonously regular music, so that in the words of choruses and refrains and in songs written closely to music it arises' (P 115–17). Prominent among his statements on the musical affinities of his poems are those on two works. He tells Bridges that *Spelt from Sybil's Leaves* 'essays effects almost musical,' further commenting, 'This sonnet shd. be almost sung; it is most carefully timed in *tempo rubato*' (LI 245–6). Comparably, in discussing *The Leaden Echo and the Golden Echo*, he tells Patmore, 'I never did anything more musical' (LIII 149). In the text he several times uses the conventional musical symbol for the pause. The marks were perhaps directed to his musician sister; he, of course, did not think of English poetry as being of a piece with pitched music.

Since the echoing well is the centre of interest and action in the poet's unfinished drama, *St. Winefred's Well*, and Hopkins describes the *Echoes* as a song designed for the drama, a highly musical treatment of the lyric text is appropriate. The musicality comes through in the text in the word and sound repetition throughout: 'No there's none, there's none, O nó there's none,' 'O there's none; no no no there's none' (lines 5, 13). The phonic quality of the sonorant *n*s contributes to the musicality of these lines in the 'Leaden Echo' section of the work, as do the sonorant *s*s and *r*s of its final lines, where 'despair' is repeated five times. The 'Golden Echo' section that follows is more than twice as long, and proportionately more complex phonically, but it is equally repetitious. It begins with 'Spare,' echoing the final syllable of 'despair' that ends the previous part, and it proceeds to verses like 'Give beauty back, beauty, beauty, béauty, back to God beauty's self and beauty's giver' (35). The final six lines culminate the verbal repetition and the build-up of sonorant *r*s and *n*s, especially in the multiple repetitions of 'fonder' and 'yonder.'

The poet's frequent use of whole word repetition is more overt here than anywhere else in his verse; it provides a test of a major charge made against his use of sound, that his concentration on sound play leads him to sacrifice verbal sense. This was one reaction to his verse from the beginning. One of his colleagues at Dublin uncharitably called his verse 'mere grammatical, acrobatic feats of juggling and word combination ... G.H. was a merely beautifully painted sea-shell. I never found any mollusc inside it of human substance' (quoted in White 386). With the verbal sense of his texts often difficult to construe, it is not surprising that similar misguided observations about his work have continued.

About the recurrent words and sounds in the *Echoes* the prominent theoretician Jonathan Culler simply admits to puzzlement at his own reaction, simultaneous feelings of rational repulsion and emotional attraction. Quoting the poem's final lines, he reports finding in them 'an excruciating ending: these four "yonders" make me shudder to recite them in public.' At the same time, Culler speaks enthusiastically of the 'séductive force' of such sounds in the poem. He notes significantly that the 'potentially mimetic' patterns in the wordplay are a 'facile and unimportant' aspect (8–9), correctly judging that onomatopoeia does not explain the poetic appeal. Nor would the current theories that Culler has extensively analysed predict his reaction, which seems a clear testimony to the independent power of the sounds of poetry.

Culler does not go beyond expressing a liking for the sounds and uneasiness with the sense. Leonard Bernstein does go further, suggesting that Hopkins is sacrificing sense to sound. In one of his compelling lectures on music at Harvard, Bernstein is intent on seeing in the *Echoes* an example of poetry approaching the status of music. He compares it to Beethoven's *Pastoral Symphony*, which has patently mimetic sounds and programmatic annotations that Bernstein sees as drawing the symphony close to verse. That view, I think, is difficult to sustain. The implicit suggestion that music and poetry exist on a single continuum sharing a broad common nature is too inclusive in the light of the differences in the sound materials and semiotic systems.

He also is mistaken in alleging that Hopkins in the *Echoes* sacrifices sense to sound. The poem, says Bernstein with compelling rhetoric, is '*almost* music, and chromatic music at that. Hopkins is wallowing in gorgeous sounds, and so are we, his readers. What is gained thereby, and what lost? What is lost is easily told: structural clarity, immediacy of meaning.' What is gained 'is an intense expressivity born of sheer sound, rich, complex, chromatic sound that doubles and redoubles in itself, creating new meanings of its own, sonorous meanings – *nonsemantic meanings*, so to speak.' Quoting the poem's last two lines, with their repetitions of 'Yonder,' Bernstein asserts, 'This ecstatic poetry has a chromaticism that leads the ear far away from the lucid, C-majorish meaning of "How to keep beauty from vanishing away?" ... Instead, the ear is led toward the new pleasures of sheer sonority, and on to bigger and better ambiguities.' He concludes: 'Phonology has virtually taken over. Syntax is all but vanished, leaving a semantic vacuum' (213–14). Attentive reading of the poetic text, however, produces good, immediately available, sense from the words. At the same time, in finding that the verbal sound carries a non-verbal musical significance, Bernstein's analysis *does* support Hopkins's theory by seeing the poetic sound as carrying independent 'non-semantic' – affective – meaning.

Bernstein's reaction is entirely sympathetic to the poet's use of sound, but probably not for reasons that Hopkins would have entirely welcomed. In the poet's notes and correspondence, he is often at pains to rationalize even his most violent compressions and dislocations of the syntax and most radical departures from customary usage. He does recognize the difficulties readers might have with certain of his works, and at one point he proposes to 'prefix prose *arguments* to some of my pieces' (LI 265), a plan he follows through on only in *Henry Purcell.* Nevertheless, the lexical meanings of his poems are not Dadaist irrationality; they finally do make sense. In support of Bernstein's claim about the *Echoes,* one might well grant that the logical meaning is attenuated, but it is hardly cancelled by the echoing reiterations. Hopkins, to be sure, sees poetry and music as close allies, but of different kinds. In his lecture notes, as I cited early in the chapter, he compares the units of poetic 'rhythm i.e. verse' to those of grammar and of music. Verse is 'the recasting of speech into sound-words, sound-clauses, and sound-sentences,' and music likewise 'is the recasting of speech used in a wide sense' (J 273).

For the poet, music offers the nearest analogy to the quantitative measure of verse. In employing identical terms to characterize music, as he did verse, as 'a recasting of speech,' he is taking the human voice as the archetypal musical instrument, and testifies to the close alliance he finds between the rhythms of the two arts. However, their differing materials – language phones and instrumental pitched sounds – dictate differing artistic methods, and they divide the two arts decisively. The poet understands that logical sense is necessary for verse, though he sees it in poetry as secondary to the intrinsically affective significance of the speech sound. Hopkins does not deal directly with the inscape of pitched music, but just as he states that 'Verse is ... speech wholly or partially repeating the same figure of sound,' so he also asserts that 'Music is composition which wholly or partially repeats the same figure of pitched sound' (J 289–90).

A semiotic analysis would agree with Hopkins that patterns of poetic sound and of pitched music are closely allied. While Charles Peirce, the originator of semiotics, never directly treats poetic sound, he does comment about the sign values of pitched music: 'The performance of concerted music is a sign. It conveys, and is intended to convey the composer's musical ideas; but these usually consist merely in a series of feelings' (1955, 277). The music, then, is taken as an image of the feelings, that is, as an icon of them. Influential philosophers of art, such as Ernst Cassirer, Charles W. Morris, and Suzanne Langer, generally accord with Peirce's iconic conception of the arts, essentially realist. Langer, writing specifically about music, calls the concept 'The most persistent, plausible, and interesting doctrine of meaning in music' (221). Hopkins's ideas about the sound patterns of verse, which he consistently presents as closely related to those of pitched music are congenial with a theory that the rhythmic patterns of both verse and music represent phonic icons of feeling.

Hopkins's poetics of speech sound identifies two types of figures of verse sound that may be repeated: there are figures that 'may be repeated runningly, continuously, as in rhythm (ABABAB),' or they may be repeated 'intermittently, as in alliteration or rhyme' (J 290). He groups devices of the second, 'intermittent,' type under the class he labels 'lettering.' I take up the important subject of lettering in the next chapter. The remainder of this chapter deals with the various types of 'continuous' repetition. Traditional metrical poetry employs three of these rhythmic divisions: foot, line, and stanza. They fit one inside the other. The foot is the fundamental unit, the basic 'speech figure' of both common and sprung rhythm: 'all rhythm and all verse consists of feet and each foot must contain one stress or verse-accent' (LII 39). Sprung rhythm feet gain life and texture through variable syllabic content, approaching 'the more picturesque irregular emphasis of talk ... making up by regularity, equality, of a larger unit (*the foot merely*) for inequality in the less, the syllable' (LIV 219; my emphasis).

Kiparsky claims that the foot is not an effective unit in Hopkins's sprung rhythm, pointing out that the poet vacillates in his instructions for analysing the feet (312). But if we review his instructions for dealing with the foot rhythm, we understand that he is aiming to facilitate performance of the verse, by taking differing approaches, rather than to define it. Writing to Canon Dixon in December 1880, Hopkins suggests that though sprung rhythm allows for 'effects or cadences, when the verse suddenly changes from a rising to a falling movement, and *this too is strongly felt by the ear*, yet no account of it is taken in scanning, but the scansion is always treated *conventionally and for simplicity*, as rising.' Further on in the letter he expatiates on Bridges's claim that in sprung rhythm 'all sorts of feet may follow one another.' He agrees, 'so they may, if we look at the *real nature* of the verse; but for simplicity it is much better to recognize, in scanning this new rhythm, only one movement, either the rising (which I choose as being commonest in English verse) or the falling (which is perhaps better in itself), and always keep to that' (LII 40 [1880]; my emphases). Varying kinds of feet are true to the 'real nature' of the verse, but 'for simplicity' the rhythm may be treated as having 'one movement.'

Despite his suggestion to Dixon that he treat sprung rhythm as having a rising movement, in his Preface three years later (1883), after having described the different kinds of foot rhythm – rising, falling, and rocking – the poet declares that while such '*distinctions are real and true to nature*,' in actual oral presentation, 'for the purposes of scanning it will be *a great convenience* to follow the example of music and take the stress always first, as the accent or chief accent always comes first in a musical bar' (P 115; my emphases). Sprung rhythm specifically 'is measured by feet of from one to four syllables ... It has one stress, which falls on the only syllable, if there is only one, or, if there are more, then scanning as above, on the first, and so gives rise to four sorts of feet, a monosyllable and the so-called accentual Trochee, Dactyl, and the First Paeon' (116). Though the instructions differ, once again he presents the adoption of a single foot rhythm as a practical convenience. A simplified analysis has natural advantages (rising emphasis is 'commonest,' falling 'better in itself'), but Hopkins also indicates that, while such analysis will serve for usual purposes, it is not, finally, 'real and true to nature.' It will presumably take a thoughtful familiarity with the individual poems to perform readily the true foot divisions in an oral presentation.

Hopkins's discussions of the metrical foot may well be unconvincing to modern analysts of English verse who question the conventional concept. But since the poet's discussions of metrics throughout his writings assume the validity of the traditional division, it is hardly possible to treat his metrical ideas without accepting its reality. Moreover, the theoretical question is hardly closed. The very fact that analysis of specific lines for which the poet has supplied complete stress notation yields some interesting possibilities suggests that foot division has a certain ontological validity.

Foot analysis seems to provide a ready way to explain apparent changes in rhythm. The culminating line of *The Windhover* is a familiar example: ['Blúe-bleak émbers, áh my déar/] Fall, gáll themsélves, and gásh góld-vermíllion' (14). The obvious crux is how to handle the abutting stresses that Hopkins marks on 'gásh' and 'góld' – single stress, double stress. There are several possibilities for dealing with the problem. Dismissing foot division, we would treat the metre as neither rising nor falling, but simply as alternating except for the abutting stresses, giving extra emphasis in reading 'góld.' A second choice would be to follow Hopkins's instructions to Dixon and read the rhythm as rising, with a minor pause before 'gold': 'I and gásh I : góld- I vermíllion.' A third would be to follow the Preface and see it as falling, with 'gásh' rather than 'góld' being a monosyllabic foot, which would leave the double stress unrationalized. But these analyses ignore what seems a sharp change in rhythm. A more satisfactory solution to the double stress on 'góld' directly after the single-stressed 'gásh' might be to assume an abrupt switch after the third foot from rising to falling: 'Fall, gáll I themsélves I and gásh II góld ver I míllion.' The shift in rhythm effectively underlines the closure of the final line.

We may find similar, if generally less striking, shifts in rhythm in a number of lines for which Hopkins marks all the stresses. (The indicated stresses are his; the foot divisions show my analysis.) He actually cites line 13 of *The Loss of the Eurydice* as an example of 'plain reversed rhythm' (LII 40), which yields, "She had cóme I from a crúise II tráining I séamen." And the poet's stress accents in *Deutschland* (line 103) (four feet) may indicate a double reversal: 'Wíry and II white-fíery I and whírlwind- II swívellèd I snów.' In this analysis the rhythm proceeds from falling in the first foot, to rocking in the second and third feet, then back to falling. In any reading the first foot must be falling (there is no slack to be 'over-rove' [LII 40] from the previous line), but to postulate that the long syllable 'white' concludes a three-syllable slack ('I Wíry and white I fíery') in the first foot is awkward; so 'white' can be attached to the next foot, producing 'I white-fíery I,' a 'rocking' amphibrach. The poet indeed states that it is characteristic of the amphibrach that its 'first short [i.e., syllable, here 'white-'] is almost long' (LI 44). Theorists might especially question the identifiability and reality of 'rocking feet,' which lack stress on both ends to mark the foot-limit, but Hopkins is confident of their reality. The suggested division of the second and third feet in this line may instance what he had in mind.

As his correspondence repeatedly attests, the poet was anxious to make his sprung rhythm more accessible to others, and his differing instructions for reading it are variously meant to achieve that practical result. That foot-measures are real he does not doubt. In answer to Bridges's complaint about his rhythms, he confidently boasts of the exactness of his rhythmic measures compared with those of other poets: 'I am stricter than you and I might say than anybody I know ... In fact all English verse, except Milton's, almost, offends me as "licentious"' (LI 44–5). At the same time, with the poet's unusual and complex rhythmic system and his emphasis on oral presentation, it does seem expedient to have a formula ready to hand for dealing with the feet, stress first probably being best. Otherwise, in the act of reading one may well lose the poetry while trying to rationalize the rhythm.

One of many testimonies to Hopkins's assiduousness in metrical construction is his profession that in his own verse he never uses the diphthongal *I* and *my* in 'short or weak' syllables, 'excepting before vowels, semi-vowels, or *r*, or when the measure is amphibrachic,' that is, rocking (LI 44). Hopkins is ever confident that he can identify the various foot scansions. He is unhesitating in pronouncing on the metrics of the choruses of *Samson Agonistes*, which have confounded many. The rhythms, he states, 'In reality ... are sprung, but Milton keeps up a fiction of counterpointing the heard rhythm (which is the same as the mounted rhythm) upon a standard rhythm ... The want of a metrical notation and the fear of being thought to write mere rhythmic or (who knows what the critics might not have said?) even unrhythmic prose drove him to this ... Milton's mounted rhythm is a real poetical rhythm, having its own laws and recurrence, but further embarrassed by having to count' (LI 45–6). Unfortunately, like Milton himself, Hopkins does not supply specific metrical analyses of *Samson*'s choruses.

Hopkins's judgment on matters such as syllable length and vowel quantity usually stands up well to more modern technical analysis, which suggests one should not lightly dismiss his postulation of the foot unit in his poetry or in that of others. Certainly, the metrical foot is essential in Hopkins's analyses of poetic sound. It is the 'rhythmic word' of verse, even as the 'bar' is 'the musical foot or word' (J 273). The units are equal to each other in phonetic quantity and strength, becoming thereby 'figures' of sound that may be repeated. Hopkins's 'figure of speech sound' in verse – foot, line or stanza – is a phonetic rather than a grammatical measure, a set of sounds characteristic of the speech of a particular language and quantitatively equal to the like figures that it is combined with. The more just the measure of the figures, the more characteristic of the language, and the more creatively varied the combinations of sounds, the more successful they will be as verse.

While Hopkins demonstrably is aware of the phonetic quantity of English sounds, it is obvious that he does not seek to make verse timing metronomic. Quite the contrary. Take lines 5 and 6 (both five feet long) from the last stanza of *Deutschland*, which I scan 'for convenience' as having falling rhythm throughout:

Let him | éaster in us, be a | dáyspring to the | dímness of us, be a |
　　crímson-cresseted | éast
More | bríghtening her | ráre-dear | Brítain, as his | réign | rólls.

The first line here, swollen by two 'over-rove' syllables at the beginning, with two six-syllable feet following, then one of five syllables and one of four, is probably Hopkins's longest five-stress line. The line following has a similar timing pattern in presenting several multi-syllabic feet preceding one or two monosyllabic feet. But within the lines the foot lengths contrast radically. To equalize them, the poet utilizes both phonetic elements, such as closed vowels and sonorant consonants, along with affective factors that could prompt the reader to lengthen or strengthen the words.

Hopkins understood well the rules of classical metrics for the composition of long and short syllables. These rules generally incorporate valid phonetic principles: for instance, long vowels or consonants that close syllables increase syllabic length. Not only did the poet read and teach Latin and Greek verse but he also composed it, and he lectured on fine points of metrics. These activities, along with his reading in the works of contemporary linguistic theorists who were applying fresh approaches to phonetics (see Milroy), no doubt stimulated his thinking about linguistic quantity. Of course, writers of his time were, by training, conscious of the distinctions of quantity in classical verse. But in accepting that English is a stress language and that stress rather than classical quantity is the basic component of English metrics, poets had often come to ignore or to pay insufficient attention to syllabic length. Hopkins sees himself as an exception among English poets in his recognition that, while stress is properly seen as the main force in English verse composition, quantity also should be a major consideration.

Hopkins often makes clear his informed understanding of phonetic length in English, as when he rejects analysis of *Fifty-two Bedford Square* as two anapests (LI 44), or speaks of the quantity of different forms of 'bid,' not only between 'bid,' 'bids,' and 'bidst,' but also between voiced and unvoiced sounds, '*bid*, with a flat dental' being 'graver or stronger than *bit*' (LII 41). He makes fine distinctions, too, in his directions to Dixon for reading sprung rhythm, in which he asserts the justice of its principle that, however many the syllables '*one stress makes one foot*' (LII 23). He states that 'if the common ballad measure allows of our having (say) in a fourfoot line "Terrible butchery, frightful slaughter" why, on principle, shd. we not say "Terrible butchery, fell swoop" and that be four feet? or further why not "Sanguinary consequences, terrible butchery"? and that be four feet? or further why not "Sanguinary consequences, fell swoop"?' (LII 22). Thus, just as 'Sanguinary' and 'swoop,' despite their differing syllable count, may readily be read as equivalent in length, so the six syllables in 'eáster in us, be a,' and four in 'dímness of us' can work as metrically equivalent to 'east,' which ends the line.

Extending the phonetic length of monosyllabic 'swoop' can make its timing equal to 'Sanguinary.' But in addition to ordinary linguistic factors that can make the feet equivalent in length, a perceptive reading can equalize them: 'In Sprung Rhythm, as in logaoedic rhythm generally,' the poet says, 'the feet are assumed to be equally long or strong and their seeming inequality is made up by pause or stressing' (P 116). To make the differing foot-lengths in these lines equivalent, he is suggesting, there are metrical occasions that demand expressive – iconic – reading. Such a reading can take advantage of phonetic features of the sounds. One phonetic feature that Hopkins applies to foot timing is the quality *continuant* applied to letter sounds whose articulation allows but does not require lengthening. Thus, he notes the various conditions in which *n* and combinations such as *ng* and *nd* may be lengthened (LII 41). In the lines from *Deutschland* quoted above, the two monosyllabic feet that conclude the second line, 'réign | rólls,' may be extended by virtue of ending in consonantal continuants; at the same time, the optional lengthening is appropriate here to the verbal sense.

Expressive factors not based on linguistic givens may be called on to equalize the feet, for example, 'pause or stressing.' Thus, line 10 of *Deutschland* ends with two monosyllabic feet, 'láshed | ród,' closed with stops (*t, d*), not continuants. It is appropriate 'to fetch out both the strength of the syllables and the meaning and feeling of the words' (P 118). It is important, furthermore, that timing can be affected by the *strength* of the stress, making the feet potentially equal through their strength, though they are unequal in real time: 'Only let this be observed in the reading, that, where more than one syllable goes to a beat, then if the beating syllable is of its nature strong, the stress laid on it must be stronger the greater the number of syllables belonging to it, the voice treading and dwelling; but if on the contrary it is by nature light, then the greater the number of syllables belonging to it, the less is the stress to be laid on it, the voice passing flyingly over all the syllables of the foot and in some manner distributing among them all the stress of one beat' (P 118). Hopkins offers as examples of increased and lessened strength the five-stress sixth line and the four-stress seventh line of stanza 31 of *Deutschland*:

Fínger of a | ténder of, O of a | féathery | délicacy, the | bréast of the |
Máiden could o | béy so, be a | béll to, | ring óf it, | and / [Stártle].

In these two lines, he says, 'the first two beats are very strong and the more the voice dwells on them the more it fetches out the strength of the syllables they rest upon, the next two beats are very light and escaping, and the last as well as those which follow in the next line, are of a mean strength, such as suits narrative' (P 118).

In stating that stress should 'fetch out both the strength of the syllables and the meaning and feeling of the words,' the poet is recognizing that the metrics need to take into account the verbal sense as well as the physical nature of the sounds. Dwelling on the first two stressed syllables, closed with nasal continuants, assists the tentativeness simulated in the words 'Fínger of a ténder of, O of a' followed by a resolution in the light, quick words 'féathery délicacy.' But the support of verbal sense remains secondary. Verse timing works with the 'natural and native' speech figure that bears emotional significance. The double change in tempo that he prescribes, from slow to fast to moderate, works with the repeating *n*s and *r*s and a rush of short syllables, 'ténder of, O of a féathery délicacy,' to create an excitement that has an analogue in the nuptial turmoil in the breast of the doomed nun (and by extension of Mary at the Annunciation). But here again, as Culler suggests of the *Echoes*, the potential mimeticism is quite subordinate to the sound value of itself. For all of his emphasis on phonetic uniformity in the metrical foot, Hopkins conceives of the uniformity as dynamic and flexible rather than lifelessly rigid. The pace of his verse varies like that of effective pitched music: 'Sprung Rhythm ... is the rhythm of all but the most monotonously regular music' (P 117).

Despite his preoccupation with the classics, Hopkins is quite conscious of the difference between classical and modern practice, in particular as regards the status of the line and stanza units. In both traditions, the foot is the basic verse figure, and with both

> The repetition of feet, the same or mixed, without regard to how long, is *rhythm*' ... A *verse* according to the ancients is a metre or piece of metre consisting of two parts divided by a *caesura* ... But in modern verse *a* verse means a complete metrical figure, a metrical unit, for as the foot is the rhythmic unit, which it repeats, so a verse is the metrical unit of repetition. It may be a *line* or a *couplet* or *triplet* or *stanza* – quatrain, octet etc. A line is an intermediate division between foot and verse, like a clause and marked off by rhyme or other means – for we must judge by the ear not by reading and the eye. (J 273)

While a line of English blank verse constitutes a 'verse,' in heroic couplets the verse is two lines, and in lyric poems like those of Hopkins, the verses are the multi-line stanzas.

The grammatical counterpart of the English verse line, according to Hopkins's is the clause; to be precise, the line is the 'rhythmic sub-clause' (J 273). His flexible handling of the sprung rhythm line accords in part with his treatment of the foot. In foot and line he aims for a reading that partially obscures the divisions. His mixing of foot types and lengths in sprung rhythm makes their underlying regularity unobtrusive, producing a cadence that simulates the irregular rhythm of natural speech; and comparably, his 'over-reeving' the line-ends hides the divisions between them while maintaining their regularity: 'It is natural in Sprung Rhythm ... for the scanning of each line immediately to take up the one before, so that if the first has one or more syllables at its end the other must have so many the less at its beginning.' The result is a stanza that is 'one long strain, though written in lines asunder' (P 116).

Many of Hopkins's feet indeed are 'over rove' from one line to the next, as in the example cited from the last stanza of *Deutschland* (lines 277–8): '| éast / More | bríghtening;' or in *Windhover* (lines 2–3), '| ríding / Of the | róll | ing.' Moreover, it is not unusual for him to 'over-reeve' the rhymes as well as the lines, as in stanza 31 of *Deutschland*, referred to above, where the rhyme of the line ending with 'breast of the' joins 'the' with the *M* of 'Máiden' at the beginning of the next line,' the/M,' rhyming with 'them' that ends two preceding lines in the stanza. And in the next line there is an even more radical rhyming of the concluding word 'and' joining with the *st* of 'Startle' – 'and/St,' rhyming with 'Providence.' However, there is an important difference between what he does with the foot and what he does with the line: though the prose-like logaoedic mixture of foot types obscures the foot-boundaries, they remain intact, while the status of the line segment as a metrical figure is genuinely compromised. The feet are isometric, but the lines are not quite isometric; between lines the slack of the last foot is often divided from the stress. The lines do maintain a fixed number of stresses, set by the stanza patterns; and the line unit is important, additionally, for supporting the rhyme scheme – the pattern of 'lettering' at line ends.

As an intermediate unit, the metrical line, the 'metre,' is equivalent to the grammatical clause; in Hopkins's terms it is the 'rhythmic sub-clause.' It does not have the primary importance of his metrical word and sentence, that is, the foot and the stanza. Nevertheless, within the fixed template of the verse form, the poet is attentive to constructing lines that are both balanced and varied, particularly in his careful orchestration of foot-patterns in each line. For instance, he places matching feet in pairs and longer sets: 'Fínger of a' is balanced by 'ténder of O of a'; and 'féathery' by 'délicacy.' And in the next line four strong stresses, each with polysyllabic slack, succeed each other (4-4-3-3-).

Four stanzas later, in the final four lines of *Deutschland* (stanza 35), we find the most impressive orchestration of foot-length and rhythm in all of Hopkins's sprung rhythm work. The fourth and third from last lines make an excellent pair structurally, if not in apparent size:

> Let him | éaster in us, be a | dáyspring to the | dímness of us, be a |
>   crímson-cresseted | éast,
> More | bríghtening her, | ráre-dear | Brítain, as his | réign | rólls.

Though the second line is palpably shorter, both lines have five feet, both begin with 'over-rove' syllables ('Let him'; 'More') with polysyllabic feet following, and both conclude with strong monosyllables ([2+] 6-4-6-5-1; ([1+] 4-2-4-1-1). This pair of lines leads admirably to the conclusion, which is in every way triumphant, not the least prosodically:

> Príde, rose, | prínce, hero of us, | hígh- | príest, |
> Oür héart's charity's | héarth's | fíre, | | oür thóughts' chivalry's |
>   thróng's | Lórd.

The two heavy monosyllables that end the preceding line (réign | rólls) put a stop to their polysyllabic rush and provide a highly effective transition to the rhythmical and syntactical complexities of the poem's two final lines, both of which also feature concluding pairs of monosyllabic feet. Indeed, Hopkins takes advantage of the natural division of the six-foot Alexandrine length of the last line to divide it in half. The echoing structure of the two halves demands a parallel scansion: each half comprises an extended six-syllable amphibrach (counting 'oür' as two syllables) that precedes the two monosyllabic feet, once more moving from polysyllables to heavy single syllables.

Another of the poet's favourite repeating structures is a series of feet, each composed of two strong syllables, with monosyllabic feet concluding the lines. A good example is line 3 of *As Kingfishers Catch Fire*: 'Stónes rìng; like | éach tùcked | stríng tèlls, | éach hùng | béll's |.' The second syllables in the first four of these feet virtually share the stress with the first syllable. I mark these with a grave accent, but perhaps shared stress would be better indicated by a bracket above the two syllables, connecting them, such as Hopkins sometimes employs to indicate 'a sort of spondee, two long syllables equally accented or nearly so, though nominally one of the two has the stress' (LI 215). Line 2 of *Duns Scotus's Oxford*, 'béll-swàr*mèd*, lárk-chàr*mèd*, róok-ràcked,' has a similar structure. The poet treats as outrides the weak syllables that interrupt the march of strong ones. The first nine lines of *That Nature Is a Heraclitean Fire* have numerous feet that are comparably made up of two strong syllables (discounting the outrides). The first line shows the pattern: 'Clóud-pùff*ball*, | tórn tùfts, | tóssed pìl*lows* | fláunt fòrth, then | chévy on an | áir- / bùilt |.'

Hopkins defends his expedient of outrides as in part compensating for the heavier phonetic length of the Italian sonnet, which he takes as a model. Outrides, he says in his Preface, 'are so called because they seem to hang below the line or ride forward and backward from it in another dimension than the line itself' (P 117). Not part of the scanning, they do not belong to the metrical units, but at the same time they contribute to the weight of the whole. By nature, he writes to Dixon, the English sonnet is 'in comparison with the Italian short, light, tripping, and trifling.' The Italian 'heavy [line] ending' and free use of elisions gives their sonnet an advantage by 'a proportion of 13:10 [syllables]' (LII 86). Hopkins, of course, also expands several of his sonnets by making the lines metrically longer – hexameter and even octameter (*Sybil's Leaves*) – and later by adding codas (*Heraclitean Fire* and *Tom's Garland*) or burden lines (*Harry Ploughman*). It is noteworthy, at the same time, that he composed numerous unexpanded sonnets that seem neither 'tripping' nor 'trifling,' especially the Dark Sonnets such as 'I wake and feel the fell of dark' and 'No worst, there is none,' using notably strong monosyllables, which are surely an advantage of the English language over the Romance languages as far as strength is concerned.

The stanza unit, the 'rhythmic sentence,' is the third and largest of the verse measures that are 'of uniform commensurable lengths and accentuations' (J 273); it is coordinate with the foot ('sound-words') and the line ('sound-clauses'). But in his own verse Hopkins handles the stanza differently from the smaller verse units. While his varying of the foot patterns from one foot to the next and his obscuring the ends of the lines and the rhyme sounds from one line to the next deliberately mask the boundaries, he nearly always points up the outlines of the stanzaic figure by making it a grammatically and logically complete statement, and in manuscript by emphasizing its integrity as a unit through prominent separation from other stanzas, using side brackets, and in the case of *Deutschland* by conspicuous numeration at each stanza's head. The stanzas often consist of several clauses, some subordinate, some coordinate, and some grammatically joined with the other clauses only by punctuation, usually semi-colons. There is no 'over-reeving' between stanzas.

Graham Storey notes that the poet's use of punctuation for his verse is 'extremely careful' (J xxx). The fact that he customarily reserves the use of periods until stanza's end is a significant confirmation of his view of stanzas as 'rhythmic sentences.' The stanza is a metrical sentence that is coextensive with a composite grammatical sentence that often combines two or more independent clauses and phrases, which are conceived as the 'sub-clauses' of the stanzaic sentence. Many of the stanzas in *Deutschland* are punctuated like stanza 2:

> I did say yes
> O at líghtning and láshed ród;
> Thou heardst me, truer than tongue, confess
> Thy terror, O Christ, O God;
> Thou knówest the wálls, áltar and hóur and níght:
> The swoon of a heart that the sweep and the hurl of thee trod
> Hárd dówn with a horror of height:
> And the midriff astrain with leaning of, laced with fire of stress.

The composite sentence here comprises three independent clauses, two marked by semi-colons (lines 2 and 4). The poet employs internal periods in only twelve of the thirty-five stanzas of the ode. In eleven of these he uses only one internal period, generally at line-end at a mid-point. But within the stanzas there is frequent terminal punctuation other than periods: semi-colons, colons, exclamation points, dashes, and question marks. Stanza 25, which has three periods, is unique. Its content is particularly dramatic: 'The majesty! What did she mean? / Breathe, arch and original Breath.'

Like the foot and line, in Hopkins's conception the stanzas constitute uniform prosodic figures that facilitate detachment of the speech inscape to the mind. A number of his mature poems consist wholly of a series of uniform stanzas, among them the odes on the sinking of the *Deutschland* and the *Eurydice, Penmaen Pool, The Bugler's First Communion, Inversnaid,* and *On the Portrait of Two Beautiful Young People.* The most interesting of these metrically, and also the most successful, is *The Wreck of the Deutschland,* with its long complex stanza form. The others are composed in short quatrains; of these even *The Loss of the Eurydice,* which Hopkins set beside *Deutschland* and Bridges preferred to it (LI 49, 119; LII 27), is undistinguished by comparison. Metrical variety seems especially important for the success of Hopkins's verse. The eight lines of the *Deutschland* stanza have a constantly changing number of beats, from two to six, while the short stanzas of the other poems have mostly short, isometric lines.

From his early Oxford days, Hopkins espoused a combination of symmetry with asymmetry in art. The professor, the authority figure in his student dialogue, 'On the Origin of Beauty,' states that beauty should be 'considered as regularity or likeness tempered by irregularity or difference,' and Hopkins prized sprung rhythm for the same quality. Like the *Deutschland* stanza, the sonnet structure that provides the verse matrix for all of Hopkins's most successful short poems in sprung rhythm represents an interesting mixture of likeness with difference. He subdivides it into successive pairs of quatrains and tercets, a symmetrical grouping of stanzas within an asymmetrical eight-six line division. In the manuscript texts of seven sonnets he points up this division by supplying side braces for each of the four units of the poems, two four-line followed by two three-line units.

It accords with Hopkins's interest in exact science that he uses an arithmetic demonstration to show how likeness and difference combine in the sonnet structure. He tells Dixon, 'The equation of the best sonnet is $(4 + 4) + (3 + 3) = 2.4 + 2.3 = 2 (4 + 3) = 2.7 = 14$.' He then proceeds methodically to expatiate on the equation's demonstration of likeness and difference (LII 71–2). Beyond locating this happy combination of likeness and difference in the sonnet proportions, Hopkins is tentative in positing the source of the form's strength. He cites Augustine's discussion in *De Musica* of uneven ratios in Latin verse such as 2:1, 3:2, 4:3, the examples being 'Hexameter and Ionic Trimeter, divided by their caesura ... so as to give the equation $3^2 + 4^2 = 5^2$.' It is indicative of Hopkins's non-mystical sensibility (see Hartman 1954, 54) that he declines to explore the potentially mystical significance of the sonnet structure that one might find in Augustine's equation; for example, the fact that $8^2 + 6^2 = 10^2$ – a perfect number squared that traditionally symbolizes divinity in Christ. But unlike medieval or Renaissance interpreters, Hopkins clearly is not engaged with potential numerological meanings. For the poet as a scientifically oriented Victorian, the aesthetic forcefulness of the simple combination of dissimilarity and likeness in the sonnet structure suffices. He well demonstrates his attachment to the core 8:6 proportion in his various expansions of the sonnet, and in the ten-and-a-half line structure of the 'curtal' sonnets (*Pied Beauty, Peace, Ashboughs*): 8:6 :: 6:4 1/2.

In his oeuvre, in accord with the strong model of sprung rhythm in

Deutschland, Hopkins's manuscript punctuation remains indicative of his conception of the stanza as a complete, typically composite, grammatical sentence, especially in his usual reserving of periods for the stanza's end and for the sonnet's divisions. In the sonnets, though, he sometimes employs exclamation marks rather than periods at points where the endings of metrical 'sentences' coincide with those of the grammatical sentence. There are notable exceptions in the later 'violent and artificial' works. In *Windhover*, the first sentence sweeps excitedly past quatrain-end all the way to a period within line 7, but exclamation points at the end of lines 8 and 11 decisively separate the octave from the sestet and divide the sestet into uniform grammatical and metrical tercets. Hopkins's stanza structures, then, bring rhythm and grammar together, thereby acknowledging that a logical statement, presented in a reasonable grammatical progression, is integral to the fully realized verse form. Nevertheless, like his conception of all formal verse elements, the stanza remains primarily a rhythmic sound structure. It is the encompassing and coordinating figure for the other repeating rhythmic units of line and foot.

The stanza unit, moreover, coordinates metrically the two main classes of figure, 'elements of verse,' that Hopkins identifies: (1) the rhythmic, marked by stress, 'which depends on strength or on length of syllable,' and (2) the rhyming, taken 'in a wide sense which depends on lettering' (J 288). As Brogan's definition of 'stanza' in *The New Princeton Encyclopedia* states, 'The notion of end rhyme and the notion of stanza are all but reciprocal.' End-rhyme 'not merely identifies line ends clearly but also produces a sound structure, a relationship among lines.' The stanza, then, is a threefold coordinator, bringing into accord the metrical patterns of speech sound with its grammatical forms, providing a container for the metrical units of foot and line, and matching patterns of verse repetition with those of rhyme repetition. The stanza, furthermore, provides the most complex unit of the metrical structure that through repetition facilitates the poetic function of 'detaching to the mind' the inscape of speech.

Rhyme repetition that reciprocally governs and is governed by the stanza is the second kind of repeating speech figure that Hopkins identifies. The role of end-rhyme in binding the stanza together is its most obvious function, but 'rhyme in a wide sense,' which the poet calls 'lettering,' includes (beyond end-rhyme) alliteration, assonance, internal rhyme, and various forms of phonetic progression. Together they have a variety of functions. The broad subject of lettering, especially in Hopkins's verse and his commentary, is my next concern.

3 Lettering: Rhyme 'Widely' Understood

The figures of rhythm, Hopkins has said, give 'more tone, *candorem*, style, chasteness' to the sound continuum of poetic speech. Rhythm purifies and brightens the figures while helping to detach the inscape to the mind. The poet similarly attributes a major function, coordinate with that of rhythm, to 'rhyme, in a wide sense,' that is, to 'intermittent' repetitions of the segmental sound figures, including end-rhyme, alliteration, assonance, vowel progressions, and similar devices, for which he coins the apt general term, *lettering*. Lettering contributes 'brilliancy, starriness, quain, margaretting' (J 290) to the speech figures. It makes the sound figures sparkle at the same time as its repetitions also help to detach the inscape. Hopkins's analysis of the nature and function of lettering is the subject of this chapter.

Hopkins's own verse makes probably the most effective use of lettering in post-medieval English verse, and it provides the best testimony for his ideas on the subject. Likewise, his insight as theorist into the function of lettering goes quite beyond that of previous writers, whose scanty formulations, generally confined to end-rhyme, are inadequate to explain the importance that the various forms of lettering have had in western verse. The poet designs the term *lettering* to remedy the ambiguity of applying 'rhyme' to all kinds of segmental repetition, its more common application being limited to end-rhyme only. He defines lettering as 'sameness or likeness of some of all of the elementary sounds – the letters – of which syllables are made' (J 283). It supplies a valuable inclusive name for all kinds of segmental recurrence.

In attributing to lettering the major active function of imparting 'brilliancy, starriness' to verse, Hopkins departs from the traditional canons of literary theory. At best, theoreticians have ascribed a regulatory function to the line and stanza defining of end-rhyme and have treated the other types of lettering as mere ornamentation. For Hopkins, however, lettering of all kinds can have an integral function in verse that is coordinate with that of rhythm. Each of the two modes illuminates verbal sound in a characteristic manner: rhythm by brightening the sound continuum, lettering by making it sparkle. A further intriguing and significant assertion for literary theory is Hopkins's statement that the 'intermittent elements of verse,' such as rhyme or lettering, make verse 'organic and what is organic is one' (J 283), taking us even farther beyond the common view of systematic lettering as of negligible import to finding in it a main contributor to coherence and unity, and to the musical – sensory – significance.

As is true of his other speculations on versification, Hopkins's concept of lettering leads him beyond treatment of its practical applications and effects, which he by no means neglects, to concern himself about its contribution to the less material effects of poetry that many critics and theoreticians, and notably poet-theoreticians, have presented as proper to it. Though systems of lettering, particularly of end-rhyme and alliteration, have been a consistent and conspicuous feature of English verse art from its beginnings, theorists since the early Renaissance have often actively deprecated their effects, especially those of end-rhyme, the most familiar form of systematic lettering. In the preface to *Paradise Lost* Milton famously speaks of rhyme as being 'to all judicious ears, trivial and of no true musical delight' (210), and most modern critics in turn have marginalized or ignored it. Typical are John L. Lowes's offhand remark that 'rhyme is, of course, an accident rather than an essential of verse' and Monroe Beardsley's summary dismissal of the device in his standard treatment of aesthetics. His inclusive survey need not deal with it, Beardsley states, since 'In English the decisive determinant of meter is stress,' not 'sound similarity' (1958, 229). Presumably there would be no other reason to treat it. Even rhyme's strongest defenders have chiefly emphasized its regulatory power rather than finding a positive contribution: for example, Dryden's influential statement that 'The labor of rhyme bounds and circumscribes an overfruitful fancy' (¶79), and John Hollander's simple assertion, in his more recent poetic *Defense of Rhyme*, that it provides line closure – 'Rhymed lines know best when to stop' (23).

The only really positive role for rhyme in poetic meaning that prominent critics other than Hopkins have asserted accords with Pope's call for verse sound to be 'an echo of the sense.' Rhyming mates have value by virtue of their semantic relationships. Thus, both the New Critic William Wimsatt and the structuralist Juri K. Lotman find sound repetitions to be without value in themselves but see importance in the relationships of the meanings of the rhymed words, in either their support for or their contrast with each other. Wimsatt asserts that 'The music of spoken words in itself is meager, so meager in comparison to the music of song or instrument as to be hardly worth discussion' (1954, 165). He compares Chaucer's 'dullish' or 'tame' rhymes with Pope's pleasurably surprising 'coupling' of incongruous or unlikely pairs (164, 158, 160). He offers a few telling examples, such as *The Rape of the Lock* (lines 105–6), in which the rhymes ironically juxtapose violation of 'Diana's *law*' of chastity with a '*flaw*' in a China jar. He declares, 'The art of words is an intellectual art, and the emotions of poetry are simultaneous with conceptions and largely induced through the medium of conceptions. In literary art only the wedding of the alogical with the logical gives the former an aesthetic value' (165). It takes logical statement to give alogical sound any poetic value. Hopkins's meaning 'over and above' the logical is thus summarily denied.

While Lotman does allow that 'we can imagine, however conditionally, a strictly musical meaning formed by relations of sound series without extra-musical bonds,' his treatment of rhyme largely agrees with Wimsatt's. He insists that attempting 'to separate sound from content' is a 'hopeless task,' since 'The musical sound of poetic speech is *also a means of transmitting information,* that is, transmitting content' (Lotman, 120); his emphasis). The effects proper to material sound are not those of logic.

In direct contrast to Wimsatt's trivialization of the 'music of spoken words' is Hopkins's effusion about the musical potential of speech. He asserts to Everard that 'the inflections and intonations of the speaking voice may give effects more beautiful than any attainable by the fixed pitches of music' (LIV 220). And instead of seeing rhyme's justification as dependent on a yoking of sound and sense, he imputes a substantial purely phonic value to verse lettering (J 290). Systems of lettering, whether those of alliteration, end-rhyme, or *skothending*, demarcate the abstract patterns of the measures, adding 'brilliancy' by means of the repeating letter sounds. Patterns of stress and intonation control linguistic emphasis and length; lettering directly implicates the fine spectrum of vowel and consonant sounds in their abstract patterns of repetition; that is, alliteration and rhyme tie the letter sounds to the rhythm. By assigning specific rhyme sounds to the stresses and measures, the segmental repetitions connect each of the sounds to the endless diversity and beauty of the physical phonic continuum; thus, in 'I cáught this mórning *mórning*'s *mínion*,' the *m*s on the stressed syllables are directly implicated in the rhythmic stress pattern.

In treating lettering in his lecture notes for 'Rhythm and Other Structural Parts of Rhetoric – Verse' (J 267–88), Hopkins discusses the leading types, distinguishing the systematic from the ad hoc. Among the systematic in the English tradition are end-rhyme, 'an agreement or sameness of sound between strong syllables in different words,' and *alliteration* or initial rhyme. Other kinds usually are 'inessential graces,' providing 'subtle beauty,' but they may be integral in the metrical systems of other languages: *skothending*, alliteration's opposite, 'ending with the same consonant but after a different vowel,' is used systematically by the Norse; likewise, *assonance*, 'sameness of vowels in syllables,' which may be called *vowelling on*, is frequently employed in Spanish verse to mark line endings. *Vowelling off*, 'changing the vowel down some strain or scale' (J 283–5), is another possibility that Scandinavian poets, in particular, exploit.

Throughout his sprung-rhythm verse and in the later sonnets especially, such as *Spelt from Sybil's Leaves* (1886) and *That Nature Is a Heraclitean Fire* (1888), the alliteration and end-rhyme coordinate with the several other forms of lettering to weave in each poem a consistent and distinctive texture of repeating sound. The sound patterns of *Sybil's Leaves*, especially, are tailored to distinctive effect, while at the same time the poem is exemplary in representing the range of the poet's lettering. In the following text I underline the alliterations on the stresses. In Hopkins's view, in accord with the Old English verse system, all initial vowels of stressed words are assumed to alliterate with each other: 'all vowels alliterate [with each other], probably because of the catch in the mouth' (J 283; cf. LIII 331–2). Thus, in the first line of *Sybil's Leaves* 'Earnest' and 'equal' are presumed to alliterate, though the *e* sounds are not the same:

> Éarnest, éarthless, équal, attúnable, | váulty, volúminous, ... stupéndous
> Évening stráins to be tíme's vást | wómb-of-all, hóme-of-all, héarse-of-all níght.
> Her fónd yellow hórnlight wóund to the wést, | her wíld hollow hóarlight
>   húng to the héight
> Wáste; her éarliest stárs, éarlstars, | stárs príncipal, óverbénd us,
> Fíre-féaturing héaven. For éarth | her béing has unbóund; her dápple is at
>   énd, as-
> Tráy or aswárm, all thróughther, in thróngs; | self ín self stéepèd and
>   páshed – quíte

Dísremémbering, dísmémbering | áll now. Héart, you róund me ríght
With: óur évening is óver us; óur night | whélms, whélms, ánd will énd us.
Ónly the béakleaved bóughs drágonish | dámask the tóol-smooth bléak light;
   bláck,
Éver so bláck on it. Óur tale, O óur oracle! | Lét life, wáned, ah lét life wínd
Off hér once skéined stained véined varíety | upon, áll on twó spools; párt,
   pen páck
Now her áll in twó flocks, twó folds – bláck, white; | ríght, wrong; réckon but,
   réck but, mínd
But thése two; wáre of a wórld where bút these | twó tell, éach off th'óther;
   of a ráck
Where, sélfwrung, sélfstrung, shéathe- and shélterless, | thóughts agáinst
   thoughts ín groans grínd.

The poet calls *Sybil's Leaves* 'the longest sonnet ever made' – that is, 'by
its own proper length' (LI 245–6). Each of its lines has eight feet,
thereby extending its 'proper length' within fourteen lines even beyond
that of his other extended sonnets, such as *Heraclitean Fire* and *Tom's
Garland* with their codas, and beyond *Harry Ploughman* with its 'burdens.'
It represents Hopkins's most intensive use of 'lettering.' In the fourteen
lines there are only four end-rhyme sounds, one being feminine, *-endous*,
and three masculine which fall consistently on monosyllabic words, *-ite*,
-ack, *-ind*. Seventy-four of the 112 stresses (66 per cent) alliterate with other
syllables in their lines. These two kinds of lettering, especially the alliteration, anchor the chiming of the word sounds throughout the poem; but
other kinds are so frequent that they become part of an inclusive system.
Take the first two lines with the various lettering underlined:

Éarnest, éarthless, équal, attúnable, | váulty, volúminous, ... 'stupéndous
Évening stráins to be tíme's vást | wómb-of-all, hóme-of-all, héarse-of-all níght.

In just these lines, in addition to the alliteration on the stresses and end-
rhyme, one finds: (1) internal rhyme on earnest and earthless, voluminous and stupendous, and the three repetitions of of-all; (2) vowel
progression ('vowelling off') in line 1 from the front -e sounds to back -o,
-au, and -u, emphasized by a progression between identical consonants,
from vaul- to vol-; and in line 2 from front to back before nasal -m: -ime,
-omb, -ome; (3) secondary alliteration between stressed 'váulty' and
unstressed 'voluminous'; and (4) skothending on -l: 'equal, attunable,
vaul-, vol-.'

Comparable variety and intensity of lettering devices continue through the sonnet. There are particularly arresting phonic effects in the matching of 'fond yellow hornlight' with 'wild hollow hoarlight' (line 3); in 'Fire-featuring' (5), and 'Disremembering, dismembering' (7); in 'beakleaved boughs,' followed by 'bleak light; black' (9), in 'our tale, O our oracle' (10), 'skeined stained veined variety' and 'part, pen, pack' (11), and in 'black, white; right, wrong; reckon but, reck but' (12), and 'selfwrung, selfstrung, sheathe- and shelterless' (14). But as much as the lettering in these individual phrases sparkles, more significant is its effect on the whole complex sound texture of the work. We might well speak of the poet's 'orchestrating' the phonic pattern.

In commenting on the work, indeed, Hopkins emphasizes its musicality, telling Bridges that it 'essays effects almost musical,' and that it 'shd. be almost sung,' having been 'most carefully timed in *tempo rubato*' (LI 245–6), which is to say that in performance certain sounds are to be lengthened and others reciprocally shortened. At the same time, the musicality is, even less than in the professedly musical *The Leaden Echo and the Golden Echo*, at the cost of the verbal sense; there is no 'wallowing,' to use Bernstein's word, in its rich sound effects. Indeed, in the powerful dramatic imagery of evening as it progresses into night, followed by a day-night contrast applied first to an eschatological metaphor for the speaker's passage from life to death, then to personal and Final Judgment, the octave represents Hopkins's most powerful externalization of the conflict between his love of the natural world's many-hued 'variety' and the stark contrast of 'black' and 'white' in his spiritual world. In the sestet, the power of blackness comes to dominate, and the poet's striving to accept the loss of the 'dapple' of the daytime world that he celebrated in earlier works like *The Windhover* and *Pied Beauty*, seems to fail in the tortured last words, in which the focus turns completely to the sufferings of the damned in hell, where 'thóughts agáinst thoughts ín groans grínd.' Happily, this bleak conclusion to his meditation on cosmic event, though the work was composed late in his life, does not represent the poet's final eschatological sentiment. That is spoken in the triumphant final coda of the even later *That Nature Is a Heraclitean Fire and of the Comfort of the Resurrection*.

In *Sybil's Leaves*, contrary to common sentence emphasis, the stresses placed on the prepositions 'agáinst' and 'ín' (line 14) contribute to the strong affective aspect that we find particularly in the later parts of the sonnet. Whereas in the first lines the stressing follows ordinary stress in the lovely and exciting objective images of earth and sky, after the middle of line 6, as the meditation becomes increasingly internalized, the speaker's emotion persistently dislocates customary stressing. Writing to Bridges about his metrical marking in general, the poet has said that either he needs to 'invent a notation applied throughout as in music or else I must only mark where the reader is likely to mistake, and for the present that is what I shall do' (LI 189). Accordingly, in *Sybil's Leaves*, Hopkins marks mainly stresses that deviate from ordinary usage, such as (I underline) 'self ín self' (6); 'dísmémbering' (7); 'óur évening,' 'ánd will énd' (8); 'óur tale, O óur oracle,' 'Lét life' (twice) (10); 'hér' and 'twó spools' (11); 'thése two,' 'twó tell' (13).

The poet instructs that *Sybil's Leaves*, 'as applies to all my verse,' should have a 'poetical (not rhetorical) recitation' (P 472). The stress markings show his (reluctant) understanding that readers would be 'likely to mistake' places where an ordinary performance would miss the emotional, 'poetical,' displacement of stress. His accent marks in the manuscript of this work make explicit the placement of stress for 59 of 112 in the poem, the greater part indicating emotional dislocation. As the poetic meditation becomes more internalized and more subjective, the relative frequency of the markings increases remarkably: in the first quatrain he supplies diacritics for only three of thirty-two metrical stresses, but in the sonnet's last four lines for twenty-eight of thirty-two.

I have said that the 'orchestration' of the sounds in this poem seems to draw to it all facets of its complex lettering. In the final analysis the underlying system is Hopkins's own, but his verse system suggests influence from three different, highly formal, vernacular systems that employ intensive lettering and with which the poet evidences familiarity. One is the Norse. In his lecture notes for 'Verse,' Hopkins speaks with admiration of Norse poetry, referring to the 'beautifully rich combination' of alliteration, skothending, and assonance in the lettering conventions. He points out especially 'use of initial and final consonant rhyme leaving out the vowel, the effect [being] that the vowels ... seem to be sided or intentionally changed, vowelled off.' He instances a stanza by Snorri Sturluson (early thirteenth century) that he found in a lecture of George Perkins Marsh. The six-syllable lines alliterate in pairs. I underline the alliteration, *skothending*, and rhyming:

Hilmir hjálma skúrir
herthir sverthi rothnu,
hrjóta hvítir askar,
hrynja brynja spángir;

hnykka Hlakkar eldar
hartha svarthar landi,
remma rimma glothir
randa grand of jarli.   (J 287)

Further, if one takes account of the lettering that carries over between lines, few of the word-sounds lie outside the lettering matrix. The Norse poets worked to display their virtuoso mastery of lettering in tour de force manipulations of the system. The complex lettering in a poem like *Sibyl's Leaves* does evoke Norse practice in a general way; nevertheless, its internal rhymes and *skothendings* are not part of a rigid system as they are in the Scandinavian work, nor are they in the first place part of a virtuoso display.

A stronger direct influence on the poet's lettering is the highly conventional sound and stress system of the Welsh known as *cynghanedd*. Hopkins loved Wales when he studied there for the priesthood (1874–7), and he made a moderately successful attempt to learn the language. He was charmed by the Welsh verse system; in commenting to Bridges in 1882 on *The Sea and the Skylark* (1877), he speaks of his Welsh days and of having been 'fascinated with *cynghanedd* or consonant chime' (LI 163–4). Hopkins even composed verse in Welsh, notably his extant poem entitled *Cywydd* after the set form of that name that celebrates the bishop of Shrewsbury's jubilee. This verse, like the Scandinavian, uses end-rhyme and an alliterative system that tends to carry over within couplets:

Y mae'n llewyn yma'n llón
A ffryddan llawer ffynon,
Gweddill gwyn gadwyd
Gan Feuno a Gwenfrewi.   (P 130)

Scholars have pointed out that the verse of Hopkins here scarcely represents strict *cynghanedd*, but it nevertheless shows a general understanding of the complex Welsh lettering system. Counting against seeing it as a controlling influence on Hopkins's verse system are not only the clear differences between the strict Welsh form and Hopkins's more flexible practice, but also the fact that he does not mention the Welsh in any of his several explanations of sprung rhythm. For a view that asserts a closer tie, see Küper (1973; 1996).

A verse system that Hopkins prominently cites in his lecture notes for 'Verse,' as well as in his correspondence and his Preface to *The Wreck of the Deutschland,* on sprung rhythm, which has been influentially put forward as a major inspiration for his poetry, is that of Old and Middle English. Yet, while Hopkins expresses a partiality to the native language and practices and cites the medieval English poets' use of alliteration as an 'essential element' in their verse (J 284), his knowledge of the languages and versification clearly was limited. Father Ong developed a comparison between the poet's sprung rhythm and Old English versification (113), but he wrote before major studies of the Old English verse that have radically changed our understanding of it were published. Thus, to meet Hopkins's claim in his Preface that sprung rhythm represents 'the rhythm of common speech and written prose,' Ong adduces the statement of the Old English scholar Kemp Malone that 'the rhythm of Old English verse grew naturally out of the prose rhythm by a process of heightening and lowering,' with its stresses and slacks coinciding with natural prose rhythms. However, neither end of Ong's comparison works. Malone's view of Old English verse has been definitively superseded, and Hopkins's statement that sprung rhythm aspires to the rhythm of 'written prose' no doubt has particular reference to the artful rhythms of classical prose, including the system of metrical *clausulae,* rather than to the plainer rhythm, represented by the 'Gettysburg Address,' that Ong adduces (see J. Wimsatt 1998, 548–50).

Like that of the Norse and Welsh, Old English versification is rigidly prescribed and has a rhythm quite distinct from modern oratorical prose rhythm. It is true that the word-class hierarchy that rules in Old English verse stress appears to posit a sense-based system: stress must fall on nouns, adjectives, and participles, not on articles, prepositions, and pronouns. Yet it is not probable that the verse grew up around the sense-stress nuclei of prose in any immediate development. Old English verse conventions developed out of practices of ancient Germanic poetry. In any event, Hopkins's evident familiarity with Old and Middle English poetry was superficial; the 'enquiring' into Old English and *Piers Plowman* that he reports to Bridges did not extend far.

At the same time, there is one set of Middle English poems that provides not an influence on Hopkins, but a particularly significant analogue to his verse practice. These works, of which *Pearl* (c. 1375) is the most notable example, combine English alliterative metrics with Romance rhyming to produce a use of lettering much like Hopkins's method 500 years later. In both verse systems the poets improvise on the traditions of lettering they found and at the same time extend them and make them flexible. The Middle English poets devise their lettering system from combining French and Italian end-rhyming with the stress-emphasis of the Middle English alliterative system. They flexibly apply the alliteration to any, all, or none of the stresses with a frequency and effect comparable to Hopkins's mature work.

In the case of both *Pearl* and Hopkins's sprung-rhythm poems the alliteration, even though it follows no rigid prescription, is the central organizer of the pattern of segmental (letter) sounds, more so than end-rhyme, which unfailingly marks each line in both works. The following is the sixth of *Pearl*'s 101 stanzas. The intensity of the alliteration in this stanza, on three-fourths of the stresses, is stronger than the average of *Pearl* as a whole (45 per cent), but it accords with the average in the first ten stanzas, where the poet is establishing the stress pattern (Cf. J. Wimsatt 1996b). I indicate the stresses by the letters above the lines, with 'A' marking the alliterating and 'X' the non-alliterating words:

    A   A   A   A
Fro spot my spyryt   ther sprang in sp<u>ace</u>;

    A   A   A   X
My body on balke   ther bod in sw<u>even</u>.

    A   A   A   A
My goste is gon   in Godez gr<u>ace</u>

    X X   A   A
In aventure   ther mervaylez m<u>even</u>.

     A   A   A   A
I ne wyste in this worlde   quere that hit w<u>ace</u>,

    A   A   A   A
Bot I knew me keste   ther klyfez cl<u>even</u>,

    X   A   X   A
Towarde a foreste   I bere the f<u>ace</u>,

     A   A   X   X
Where rych rokkez   were to dyscr<u>even</u>.

     A   X   X   A
The lyght of hem   myght no mon l<u>even</u>,

```
      A      A         X    A
The glemande glory    that of hem glent;
```

```
      A        A         A    A
For wern never webbez   that wyghez weven
```

```
  X      A      A    X
Of half so dere   adubbement.
```

While in both Hopkins's poems and *Pearl* the complexity of the rigid end-rhyme system is notable, it is the flexible alliterative scheme that provides the main organizational focus for the pattern of segmental sound. The alliteration at the same time strengthens the stresses significantly. The versification of the two poets' works, historically unrelated, are finally linked by the sheer effect of their lettering. They constitute significant empirical evidence for the potential power of poetic sound – and notably alliteration in English – to assume overriding importance with different poets in differing traditions.

Like the Pearl Poet's work, composed at the height of the fourteenth-century Alliterative Revival, Hopkins's intensive lettering for his sprung-rhythm verse has manifold predecessors that provided models, but it is very much his own synthesis. He employs almost exclusively the conventional end-rhymed forms of the sonnet and homostrophic ode, both of his patterns having antecedents in Milton. As is standard, his end-rhyme schemes mark the divisions of the stanzaic 'metres' into lines, with the completion of the scheme signalling the end of the stanza. End-rhyme is important, then, in delineating the verse structure and also for its participation in the lettering through tying in specific segmental (i.e., letter) sounds with the texture of the phonic continuum. We may instance the major function of end-rhyme in the opening quatrain of *Windhover* (in identifying the stresses I follow the poet's marking and, in its absence, a consensus of commentators; the vertical lines suggest foot divisions):

I cáught this | mórning | mórning's | mínion | kíng-
          dom of | dáylight's | dáuphin dapple-| dáwn-drawn | Fálcon in his |
          ríding
    Of the | rólling level | únder | néath him steady | áir, and | stríding
Hígh there how he | rúng upon the | réin of a | wímpling | wíng ...

The rhyme word of the first line, 'king-,' provides a key sound for the octave. It picks up and stresses the '-ing,' sounded twice previously unstressed in 'morning'; and it initiates the eightfold rhymes on '-ing,' which alternate stressed with unstressed in the octave: 'ríding,' 'stríding,' 'wíng,' then 'swíng,' 'gliding,' 'hiding,' and 'thing.' As is always the case, the more pervasive the chiming, the more it implicates the rest of the sound pattern. Here the sound echoes extend to the -ngs of line-internal 'rólling,' 'wímpling,' 'and 'rúng,' and further to the numerous ns, in 'dáwn-drawn falcon,' etc.

End-rhyme is the rigid aspect of Hopkins's lettering system. But it is the flexible alliteration that has particular potency in imparting to the stress sounds the special brilliance of pearls, to use his synaesthetic comparison. At the beginning of *Windhover*, the 'starriness' that the poet also attributes to lettering literally suits the word meanings: the brightness of the 'morning,' the 'daylight,' and the 'dawn'; Christ's glory in 'morning's minion,' 'king-,' and 'dauphin.' The lettering, one might think, generates the verbal sense; its general function in sprung rhythm, of course, is in the phonic context, in giving vital prominence to the stresses, the 'life' of sprung rhythm. All sprung-rhythm stresses require clear identity, and some need extra emphasis, as Hopkins specifies in his 'Preface' to *Deutschland*: 'Only let this be observed in the reading, that, where more than one syllable goes to a beat, then if the beating syllable is of its nature strong, the stress laid on it must be stronger the greater the number of syllables belonging to it' (P 118).

Alliteration is Hopkins's favoured way of adding prominence to the stresses. Its position at the onset of the word or syllable makes it uniquely effective in building them up. As a result, though alliteration is not requisite in any particular position in Hopkins's sprung rhythm, its faculty of imparting stress emphasis makes it central to the efficacy of his system, the most essential aspect of the lettering. In his lecture notes on verse Hopkins says of alliteration, 'one may indeed doubt whether a good ear is satisfied with our [English] verse without it' (J 284), and a statistical analysis of his use of it in sprung rhythm suggests its importance to the effect.

In *Sybil's Leaves*, as I have noted, 66 per cent of the stresses (74 of 112) alliterate with other stresses in their lines. This is somewhat more than the average in the bulk of his sprung-rhythm verse. By my count, of the 1,120 stressed syllables in *Deutschland*, 626 or 55.9 per cent alliterate with stresses within their lines, and of 960 stressed syllables in twelve of his most popular sprung-rhythm sonnets, 557 or 58.0 per cent similarly

Table 3.1. Hopkins's Alliterations

Alliteration on the primary stresses within the lines of selected poems

Short title	No. Lines	No. Stresses	Stresses Allit.	Per cent Allit.
Homostrophic odes				
Deutschland	280	1120	626	55.9
Eurydice	120	450	193	42.9
Twelve sonnets in sprung rhythm				
Windhover	14	70	38	54.3
Pied Beauty	10½	42	28	66.7
Caged Skylark	14	70	41	58.6
Scotus's Oxford	14	70	41	58.6
Henry Purcell	14	84	53	63.1
Kingfishers	14	70	43	61.4
Sybil's Leaves	14	112	74	66.0
Carrion Comfort	14	84	41	48.8
No Worst	14	70	37	52.9
I Wake and Feel	14	70	43	61.4
Harry Ploughman	19	86	49	56.9
Heraclitean Fire	24	132	68	51.4
Sonnet totals	179½	960	557	58.0
Two early poems in 'standard' rhythm				
Heaven-Haven	8	26	8	30.8
Habit of Perfection	28	112	34	30.4
Two mature sonnets in 'standard' rhythm				
God's Grandeur	14	70	43	61.4
Starlight Night	14	70	41	58

alliterate. In table 3.1 (from J. Wimsatt 1998), I do not count alliterations that run over from one line to the next, though these occasionally are important.

The poet had certainly cultivated alliterating effects before he formulated sprung rhythm. As table 3.1 shows, in his early *Heaven-Haven* and *Habit of Perfection*, more than 30 per cent of the stresses alliterate, but these are usually in set phrases like 'double dark' rather than involving the extended line patterns:

Be shellèd, eyes, with <u>d</u>ouble <u>d</u>ark
And find the uncreated light:
This <u>r</u>uck and <u>r</u>eel which you remark
<u>C</u>oils, <u>k</u>eeps and teases <u>s</u>imple <u>s</u>ight.   (*Habit of Perfection*, 9–12)

The sprung rhythm norm, by contrast, involves almost twice as much alliteration, often with complex interweaving. A comparison of the two odes yields another statistic attesting to the contribution of alliteration: *Deutschland*, the poet's masterpiece and practical program for the rhythm, has a substantially greater percentage (55.9) of alliterating stresses than does the much less successful *Loss of the Eurydice* (42.9).

Stress is the 'life' of sprung rhythm because it is the central feature of the 'natural rhythm of speech' and at the same time is central in English metrical rhythm. The bringing together of the stresses of normal speech and of metre, which 'one wd. have thought incompatible' (LI 46), is sprung rhythm's triumph. Alliteration's strengthening of the stresses both promotes the alliance of the verse with the 'current language' and helps to define the metrical structure. Alliterating phrases ('ruck and reel,' 'double dark,' 'simple sight') mark natural speech, and Hopkins's sprung-rhythm work greatly intensifies this feature: 'The poetical language of an age shd. be the current language heightened, to any degree heightened and unlike itself' (LI 89). Other poets, of course, have invoked the necessity of using 'current language.' We might compare the statements of two others in particular whose verse aims at a similar goal and does not employ such intensive lettering.

In the first instance, Hopkins's commentary about the language of sprung rhythm evokes Wordsworth's statements in the 'Preface' to the *Lyrical Ballads*, where the great Romantic declares that he has aimed to fit 'to metrical arrangement a selection of the real language of men in a state of vivid sensation,' to present his verse 'in a selection of language really used by men.' In invoking speech usage, the two poets express themselves quite comparably, yet the poetry of the two strongly contrasts, and it would seem that Wordsworth had much better success in capturing the current language, even in his rhymed verse. Compare the overtly strange, 'I caught this morning, morning's minion, king- / dom of daylight's dauphin, dapple-dawn-drawn Falcon' or 'Earnest, earthless, equal, attunable' (*Sibyl's Leaves*) with the opening of the *Intimations of Immortality* ode, one work of Wordsworth that Hopkins unreservedly admired:

There was a time when meadow, grove, and stream,
The earth, and every common sight,
    To me did seem
   Apparelled in celestial light,
The glory and the freshness of a dream.

Wordworth's expression hardly has the naturalness of prose throughout. In line 3, instead of 'To me did seem,' 'Seemed to me' would be more like ordinary language, and in four 'Dressed' would be more usual than 'Apparelled'; but Hopkins's syntax ('this morning morning's,' 'dapple-dawn-drawn') and diction ('minion,' 'wimpling') surely present much less ordinary English locutions. An important point of distinction is that, whereas Hopkins speaks of speech *rhythms*, Wordsworth's statement suggests common diction and phraseology adjusted to a fixed 'metrical arrangement.' The one poet espouses the natural rhythms of language, *however heightened* (LI 89; my emphasis), the other the usage of ordinary people adapted to traditional verse structure. Yet there abides their common aim to utilize current language.

We might find a midpoint, if not a common denominator, between the formulations of the two poets in the theoretical statements of a third, T.S. Eliot. In his essay, *The Music of Poetry*, Eliot sounds more like Words-worth than Hopkins in speaking of 'the law that poetry must not stray too far from the ordinary everyday language which we use and hear' (13). Accordingly, when discussing Hopkins, Eliot has some difficulty in accommodating his poetry to 'everyday language,' though he tries. He grants that the poems 'may sound pretty remote from the way in which you and I express ourselves ... but Hopkins does give the impression that his poetry has the necessary fidelity to *his* way of thinking and talking to himself' (20). This is lame, for what Hopkins says to himself may or may not be 'the ordinary everyday language which we use and hear.' At the same time, Eliot's very subject, the 'music of poetry,' which he defines as 'a music latent in the common speech of its time' (17), brings him closer to Hopkins the theorist of prosody who speaks, not of diction and syntax, but of 'the native and natural rhythm of speech.' Like Hopkins, Eliot foregrounds the 'speech rhythms and sound patterns' of language (27).

Yet Eliot as poet, rather than standing at a midpoint, often seems positioned at the third corner of a triangle, equally far from both Wordsworth's and Hopkins's verse:

O the moon shone bright on Mrs. Porter
And on her daughter
They wash their feet in soda water

Et O ces voix d'enfants, chantant dans la coupole!

Twit twit twit
Jug jug jug jug jug jug
So rudely forc'd.
Tereu.   (*Waste Land* 199–206)

A melange of rhythms here mingles with highly allusive and macaronic phraseology to produce what seems anything but ordinary speech usage. The example, of course, is extreme; elsewhere Eliot sounds much more colloquial. In any event, whatever the differences between the three poets' verse, their very success as poets and their acuity as theorists give one some confidence that a truth genuinely lies behind each of their generalizations about the language of poetry. Wordsworth in 1800, Hopkins in 1883, and Eliot in 1942: each in his own formulations invokes what Eliot calls the 'music latent' in current speech (1942, 27).

The common factor, it seems, is that all three poets are aiming at a poetical rather than a mimetic naturalness, one that resides in the rhythms more than in idiomatic phraseology – in Wordsworth's 'metrical arrangement,' in Eliot's 'natural rhythm.' In these terms Hopkins's use of alliteration is his way of achieving naturalness, by heightening the stress of the current language. The intensive alliteration performs the important function of poetically concentrating the stress, the element that particularly characterizes the rhythms of 'ordinary modern speech' (LI 89).

Alliteration, I have noted, is the central device among the several devices of lettering that occur in abundance in Hopkins's sprung rhythm works. It can be important for both primary and secondary stresses, along with end-rhyme, mostly a given as well as pervasive internal rhyme, *skothending*, vowelling on (assonance), and vowelling off. All add to a systematic enhancement of the stresses and are instrumental in producing the poet's grand variety of sound textures in his different works. *Sibyl's Leaves* makes particular use of assonance and vowel gradation. The lettering has another emphasis in *As Kingfishers Catch Fire*, which I cited in chapter 2 for its use of secondary stresses. Here, interwoven alliteration on both primary and secondary stress builds lines that are particularly strong phonically. (In the following I underline the alliteration and suggest foot-divisions):

> As k̲íngfishers | c̲átch f̲ire | d̲r̲ágonf̲lìes | d̲ráw | f̲láme;
> As | túmbled | óver | r̲ím in | r̲óundy | wélls |
> S̲tónes rìng; like | e̲ach t̲ùcked | s̲tríng t̲èlls, | e̲ach hùng | béll's |
> B̲ów swùng | f̲índs tòngue to | f̲líng òut | b̲róad its | náme.

Taking into account both degrees of stress, the first line alone yields the impressive repetitive pattern of alliteration, k-f | k-f | dr-f | dr- | f, implicating all eight of the primarily or secondarily stressed syllables. In lines 3 and 4 the internal rhymes of 'ring' with 'string,' 'tells' with 'bells,' echoing 'wells,' and 'swung' with 'tongue,' echoing 'hung' in the previous line, along with six *skothendings* on *-ng*, strengthen the stressed-word sounds. In Hopkins's terms all of the lettering devices add jewel-like brilliance at regular points in the sound continuum. Nevertheless, the remarkable coherence of the effect in the whole poem is, in the first place, dependent on alliteration on the stresses, the aspect of lettering that most unifies and gives force to the organization of sound generally in Hopkins's sprung rhythm verse.

In his lecture notes for 'Verse' (1874), Hopkins had adumbrated the importance that lettering was to assume in his practice of sprung rhythm, which was incubating in his mind at that time. Rather than seeing lettering as producing simply a mechanical coherence and unity through marking abstract patterns of stress and measure, he calls on the image of organic unity inherited from the Romantics. The 'intermittent elements of verse, as alliteration, rhyme,' he asserts, 'do not break the unity of the verse but the contrary; they make it organic and what is organic is one.' To elucidate the always problematic notion of organicism that he has introduced, he offers another rather enigmatic metaphor: 'All the parts of water are alike but the parts of man's body differ and man's individuality is marked but the individual being [that] a water drop has is gone when it falls into the water again' (J 283). He means, I take it, that rhythm marked only by random, unassociated segmental sounds tends to have a sameness of parts comparable to inorganic water; however, the repetition of specific segmental stress sounds, lettering, imparts to the phonetic components individual identity, connecting the parts while differentiating them like the organic constituents of a man's body. Hopkins's metaphor has the considerable advantage of indicating that while stress by itself is vital to sprung rhythm, the connection of the abstract stress pattern with the specific sound continuum by means of the repetitions of lettering integrates the segmental patterns with the suprasegmental or 'prosodic' elements of language. Stress alliteration, then, emphasizes the stresses while associating them with the phonic and linguistic continuum, conducing to 'organic' unity.

Hopkins does not pursue the organic metaphor's biological sugges-tiveness to further characterize the poetic unity that he envisions, but rather he introduces a geometric image, that of pi – the ultimately indeterminable ratio of a circle's circumference to its radius: 'In every-thing the more remote the relationship of the parts to one another or the whole the greater the unity if felt at all, as in the circle and ellipse, for the circle is felt to be more at one and one thing than the ellipse, yet the ratio of its circumference to its diameter is undiscoverable, whereas there must be one ellipse in which it is 3:1 and any number of others in which it is any ratio we like between pi and 2' (J 283). While the organic metaphor indicates how lettering does not 'break,' but rather marks rhythm and increases its unity, the circle and ellipse comparison suggests that the complications of lettering carry the poem beyond the arithmeti-cally simple uniformity of abstract rhythm that is unmarked by lettering, which is the unity of the ellipse, to a unity that is 'more remote' and 'undiscoverable' but 'more at one,' that is, the circle.

As the organic metaphor suggests, lettering adds complexity and interest to a poem's sound pattern, making its parts at the same time distinctive and coherent and unified. The circle and ellipse comparison asserts, in invoking the mystery of pi, that lettering, rather than being a mechanical element of verse subject to simple analysis like the ellipse, provides a unifying complication that makes it analysable only on its own terms like the circle. In Hopkins's view, as I will discuss in chapter 5, these 'terms' of poetic sound that provide the basis of its characteristic signification involve a 'prepossession of feeling,' sensory and emotional. The rhythms of native and natural speech sound convey emotion, as do the rhythms and repetitions of metrical language. Stress is central, mark-ing the place where natural speech sound and metrical sound come together. Alliteration strengthens the impact of their meeting.

Hopkins employs lettering, alliteration most centrally, to give a re-markable phonic complexity to his sprung rhythm verse. In order to understand how this complexity contributes to the emotional force of this verse, we might invoke T.S. Eliot's intriguing doctrine, which states that an 'objective correlative,' an embodiment of feeling, potentially may be inherent in an art work: 'The only way of expressing emotion in the form of art is by finding an "objective correlative"; in other words, a set of objects, a situation, a chain of events which shall be the formula of that *particular* emotion; such that when the external facts, which must terminate in sensory experience, are given, the emotion is immediately evoked' (1949, 387). The facts lead to a sensory experience, which evokes the emotion. Instead of objects, situations, or chains of events, we might suggest that Hopkins offers a complex organization of sounds as the 'formula' of the emotion. The idea that the patterning of verbal sound can have important emotional content is supported by the profoundly emotional effects of pitched music, another form of patterned sound.

Literary theorists have often criticized Eliot's famous formulation, mainly because of the indistinct role that he attributes to emotion (see, e.g., Vivas). Eliot's subject is the dramatic action of *Hamlet*. In lyric poetry, especially Hopkins's lyrics, the primacy of the role of emotion is much more obvious than it is in drama, and is perhaps more susceptible to understanding in terms of Eliot's 'correlative.' To lend some specificity to the search for the emotional prepossession of speech that Hopkins speaks of, we might look at another lengthy sonnet, *That Nature Is a Heraclitean Fire and of the Comfort of the Resurrection*, whose sounds correlate with poetic representation first of pagan philosophical excitement and later of a deeper Christian ardour. The work's 'many outrides and hurried feet' and the 'two codas' (P 493; actually, three codas) that the poet identifies are indicative of the work's emotional overflow. In accord with Heraclitus's doctrine of continuous flux, the poem's first quatrain presents Nature as a dynamic cosmic 'bonfire' (In striving to follow the poet's marks, I suggest primary and secondary stresses, underline the alliterations of both, separate the feet, and italicize the outrides):

Clóud-pùff*ball*, | tórn tùfts, | tóssed pìll*ows* ‖ fláunt fòrth, then | chévy on
   an | aír-
bùilt | thórough*fàre* : | héaven-ròy*sterers*, in ‖ gáy-gàngs they | thróng;
   they | glítter in | márch*es*.
Dówn ròugh*cast*, | dówn dàzzling | whíte*wàsh*, ‖ wheréver an | élm | árches, |
Shíve*lights* and | shádowtàckle in lóng ‖ láshes lace, | lánce, and | páir.

Exhilaration characterizes the sound in this quatrain, which seems to be born in the author's feeling of elation as a cosmic observer, and, as with pitched music, communicates the inherent feeling to the auditor. The powerful nuclear stresses are at the heart of the effect. The forceful beat, emphasized by series of matching feet with secondary stress, the heavy punctuation, and especially the alliterations combine to produce a strong staccato, made up of quick, excited sets of short syllables. Hopkins's poetics suggests that the verbal music produced by the sound pattern provides the immediate 'objective correlative' of the emotion represented. The representation of the evanescence of all phenomena of the cosmos attendant on the sounds extends this correlative to verbal meaning.

But the lines of *Heraclitean Fire* that follow the quatrains quench the excitement. The poet switches from a cosmic to a personal viewpoint and meditates on the melancholy consequences that the Heraclitean view implies for man's extraordinary person: 'Man, how fast his firedint, his mark on mind, is gone!' (11). Then, in another reversal, the consolation of Christ's incarnation intervenes. The denouement is even more emotional and dramatic than the opening. The last coda has short linking and final lines:

> In a flásh, | at a trúm | pet crásh,
> I am áll | at ónce | what Chríst is, || since hé was | what Í am, | ánd |
> This Jáck, | jóke, | pòor pótsherd, | pátch, | mátchwòod, im | mórtal |
>   díamond, |
>   Ís im | mórtal | díamond.   (21–4)

Here the strong alliterations are assisted by notable internal rhyme and vowel gradation to give particular effect to the stresses. The brief appositions and the monosyllabic feet in the third line particularly implement the phonic excitement.

The importance of stress to sprung rhythm also brings Hopkins's idiosyncratic use of sound into accord with the formulation of Robert Frost (invoked in chapter 1), whose verse achieves quite different phonic effects. Rejecting the notion that 'the music of words [is] a matter of harmonized vowels and consonants,' Frost demands that verse manifest 'the sound of sense.' Much like Hopkins, what he suggests is not a close marriage of sound with specific meanings, but rather an independent speech music abstracted from specific verbal sense. His description of it as 'the sound of sense' in voices heard from behind a door is especially apt to Hopkins's poetics of speech sound (Frost 1973, 58–9). The stressed sounds, of course, are what the voices convey most clearly, whether they are speaking excitedly of a 'trumpet crash' in *Heraclitean Fire*, or calmly in Frost's meditative *Birches*: 'One could do worse than be a swinger of birches' (line 60).

The verse sounds of Frost and Hopkins, despite strong differences in their phonetic patterns, are – as Hopkins and Eliot (1942, 17) instruct they should be – apt to their time and place. Frost's iambic beat pulses with New England accents, Hopkins's irregular inflections with Germanic and Celtic cadences. Seamus Heaney, in a comment quoted in chapter 1, finds in his own early verse a kinship with Hopkins's 'bumpy' rhythm, specifically seeing the connection to reside in native speech sounds (1980, 44). Frost's lettering, by contrast, is muted. His consistent end-rhyming is unobtrusive: 'Whose woods these are I think I know. / His house is in the village, though,' and his restrained alliterating is anything but 'bumpy': 'Nature's first green is gold, / Her hardest hue to hold' (*Stopping by Woods*, lines 1–2; *Nothing Gold*, lines 1–2). Though Frost often makes effective use of lettering, mainly in end-rhyme, it is by no means essential to the success of his more extended poems.

By contrast, it is hard to imagine Hopkins achieving his impressive phonic effects without lettering, but he obviously did not think lettering generally requisite for successful verse. He admired and emulated above all the most notable English detractor of rhyme, Milton; and his eclectic praise of many different poets, rhyming or not, testifies that he would agree with Eliot that various poetic techniques can be effective so long as the necessary connection is made with the current language: 'Whether poetry is accentual or syllabic, rhymed or rhymeless, formal or free, it cannot afford to lose its contact with the changing language of common intercourse' (Eliot 1942, 13). The essential element for both poets is rhythm, whose significance is not bound to the verbal sense and may precede it. As Eliot says, 'I know that a poem, or a passage of a poem, may tend to realise itself first as a particular rhythm before it reaches expression in words, and that this rhythm may bring to birth the idea and the image' (28). Hopkins's statements about verse and inscape posit much the same kind of preverbal development. For him, the origin of the nascent poem is in a 'prepossession of feeling,' which becomes embodied as 'inscape of spoken sound, not spoken words.' Comparable to pitched music, then, its verbal music conveys an originary sensory and emotional significance that is over and above its 'grammatical, historical, and logical meaning' (J125, 289).

Hopkins no doubt overstates the case in positing that alliteration may

be essential in English poetry to 'satisfy the ear' (J 284). But it is undoubtedly a vital element in the success of sprung rhythm, particularly in
its identifying and emphasizing the stress. While the rhythms of poets
such as Frost or Tennyson are based mostly in a more or less regular
alternation of stressed and unstressed syllables, in sprung rhythm the
placement of stresses is quite variable. They may be adjacent or separated by one to three or even more syllables. Alliteration is a great
facilitator of the triumph of sprung rhythm in making the rhythms of
artful verse accord with those of natural speech. It assists the stress and
often makes clear where it falls.

Lettering, particularly alliteration in Hopkins's mature poetry, makes
palpable the unity of the foot and its 'organic' phonic nature by bringing
out the stress, which in English is 'more *of* a stress' and basic in the
speech rhythm of the language. It is a major element, furthermore, in
the poet's framing of verse units of uniform length and strength, which
set up repetitions that '*often*,' '*over-and-over*,' and '*after*' the inscape for
the 'contemplation' of the poetic audience. Such contemplation brings
out the inscapes – the inner forms or patterns – of the word-sounds. For
Hopkins, nevertheless, the rhythmic repetitions do not act as mystical
mantras leading to heavenly insight, as the term 'contemplation' might
suggest. Instead, the extraordinary variety of the sound repetitions leads
the auditor to hear the veritable *rhythm* of current speech, which bears
importantly on the affective significance that is the essence of poetry.

In Hopkins's view patterned sound, conveying independent emotional content, is the main basis of poeticalness, that which separates
poetry from rhetoric. Verse's repetition of sound figures generally is
requisite in conveying to the auditor's perception of inscape in a verbal
music that is parallel in character to that presented by pitched music; the
semiotic effect of this music arises prior to the explicit verbal sense.
Seamus Heaney expresses comparable ideas about verbal music a number of times in his essays, as in his lecture 'The Makings of a Music:
Reflections on Wordsworth and Yeats,' where he speaks of his interest in
'the relationship between the almost physiological operations of a poet
composing and the music of the finished poem,' and of his desire 'to
explore the way that certain postures and motions within the poet's
incubating mind affect the posture of the voice and the motion of
rhythms in the language of the poem itself.' He seeks 'the origins of a
poet's characteristic music' (1980, 61). If, as other prominent poets
join him in suggesting, the rhythmic music of the words is felt anteced-
ent to the lexical meaning, that constitutes compelling testimony for

the independent significance of the sounds of poetry. Moreover, the very success of Hopkins's sprung-rhythm poems, with the powerful effects of their sounds, provides an excellent empirical justification for the poet's predilection for the complex phonetic patterning that the alliteration organizes.

4 'Inscape' and Poetic Meaning

Literary critics commonly have agreed that the significance of poetry reaches beyond that of its lexical and grammatical meaning. But these analysts mostly assume that the exact nature of poetry's special significance is muffled under an impenetrable mystical veil: reading poetry, one hears the 'wingbeats of the unknown,' as George Steiner has it, but Steiner leaves the source of the wingbeats pleasantly mysterious. Hopkins, however, an inveterate theorist, does not circle around the problem. Much like a Scholastic philosopher, he has faith that even the latent significance of the patterns of human speech sound may be approached by way of metaphysics.

As an artefact made up of material sound, poetry for him has a veiled significance related to that of the clouds and trees and waves whose physical designs Hopkins intensely scrutinizes when he walks out in the countryside. His interest in his observations is in discerning the cosmic patterns behind the forms. He calls such patterns the *inscape*. And just as he speaks of an Alpine glacier that is 'swerved and inscaped strictly to the motion of the mass' (Brown 231), thereby indicating aspects of its inner structure, so too his theory holds that poetry can discover – uncover – deep affective meaning in patterns of human language sound. To be sure, a context of language meaning is requisite: 'Some matter and meaning is necessary,' but such meaning has only an ancillary function as 'an element necessary to support and employ the shape which is contemplated for its own sake' (J 289). 'Contemplation,' signifies for him an 'abiding kind' of expense of mental energy in which 'the mind repeats the same energy on the same matter' (J 126).

The matter that the contemplation of the 'shape' (i.e., scape, pattern) aims to settle on is the inscape, which Hopkins identifies as 'the very soul of art' (LII 135). It is the central term of his personal metaphysics. In this chapter, I call on the poet's diaries, verse, and particularly his theoretical writings to elucidate his concept and, further, to specify so far as possible how inscape is manifested in the repeating speech-sound figures. My understanding of inscape, in line particularly with Louis Mackey's discussion of John Duns Scotus and Hopkins, is that the poet arrived at his concept as a result of his belief in philosophical realism, and that he found a full explanation and justification of it in Duns Scotus's version. Inscape comprises the universals, the *real generals* that realism hypothesizes lie behind the particularity of individual phenomena. Duns Scotus calls the generals *formalities*, and the particularity *haecceity* (thisness). Hopkins's realism and Scotus are a main topic throughout this chapter.

Hopkins asserts that poeticalness is based on the inscape of patterns of material speech sound. Patently, he conceives of this meaning as essential to language, part of intrinsic language significance. Such meaning, nevertheless, since it is dependent on material sound, is outside the purview of what is today the most widely accepted theory of language, which holds that properly linguistic meanings, those shared by a language community, are only the meanings determined by systematic phonemic contrasts. Other significances are not shared, are not linguistic. The sensations and feelings conveyed by the sound units, their continuums, and their emphases do not have properly linguistic meaning beyond the logical and grammatical sense that contrastive sounds – phonological contrasts – produce.

Charles Sanders Peirce's 'Semiotics' is more hospitable to Hopkins's concept that accords to material pattern of sound a linguistic significance in revealing the inscape of speech sound. Peirce was a wide-ranging scientist and philosopher, and his theory of signs provides for the sign value of all phenomena that are taken by an observer as meaningful; it recognizes the existence of many sign systems. A bird's song bears semiotic meaning for other birds of the same species. Human languages are simply the most complex of sign systems. Semiotics sets up three classes of sign value: symbol, index, and icon. The 'symbols' of semiotics are those of the scientist (e.g., Cu for copper), not those conventionally found in literature ('O, my love is like a red, red rose'). While the symbolic is primary, language makes use all three kinds; indeed, most word signs can embrace iconic, indexical, and symbolic value.

Peirce's symbols cover meanings produced by the arbitrary matching of sound and sense; they are produced by sound contrasts alone, and are not connected directly with the material sound. On the other hand, the significances of verbal index and icon arise directly from that sound. Sound icons are central to Hopkins's idea of poeticalness. Icons are sensory images that carry meaning by virtue of resemblance: the image of a tiger used in a gasoline company's advertisements acts as a visual icon signifying power; the ads imply that like the tiger, the gasoline is powerful. Similarly, the sound of chimes heard on a Sunday morning is an aural icon evoking the image of a church service (also indexically pointing to the service). Particularly important for Hopkins's concept of poetry are emotional intonations and emphases and word sounds in their context and history, which also can carry iconic significances that are systematic for many in a language community. In the main they are not the ad hoc product of a single speaker.

When present, the iconic meanings of word sounds generally exist in addition to the symbolic sense that word-sound contrasts carry. Onomatopoeia provides obvious examples of such iconic meaning. 'Crack,' for instance, is a conventional English *symbol* that the language system employs whose arbitrarily fixed sense depends on a multitude of phonetic contrasts with other word symbols, including 'sack,' 'back,' 'crank,' 'crane,' and so on. But at the same time its sound tends to evoke the material sound that is associated with the breaking of something brittle. It thereby also acts as a sound *icon.*

In Hopkins's terms simple onomatopoeia and other mimetic language sound meanings are part of the scapes, not necessarily a force in poetic inscape, which concerns iconic sign meaning beyond the scapes: *inner* meanings. For a Scotistic realist such inner meaning involves *real generals,* universals. When Hopkins tells Bridges that love is 'the great moving power' of poetry (LI 66), in terms of his realism he is imputing to that which the word *love* in some approximation represents: a real, not simply lexically convenient, existence. For Hopkins, then, one or more of the formalities that love comprises carries the power to motivate poetry, and we may suppose it to be part of the inscape of a poem.

Hopkins's discussion of the properties of a word in his untitled student essay, 'All words mean things or relations of things,' suggests that inscape is the poetical feeling that is inscribed in the sound figures prior to the lexical meanings. Its significance is precedent to that of the verbal (symbolic) representation. One may compare the prior ranking to a judgment that with a painting the artistic significance of the expressive ordering of the physical materials, its patterns of line and colour, carries its inscape, ranking ahead of the success of its representation. Abstract art makes such an assumption.

Clearly, more is involved in inscape than the physical sound *of itself.* Materialism is wholly foreign to Hopkins's disposition and to his studies at Oxford, especially of Greek idealism under Benjamin Jowett and T.H. Green. The main evidence of what he drew from this undergraduate study consists of several essays that survive from that time, including 'The Position of Plato to the Greek World' (1865; written for T.H. Green), 'The Probable Future of Metaphysics' (1867), and two short papers on the history of Greek philosophy that are especially valuable for under-standing his linguistic ideas: the first the untitled piece, 'All words ...,' composed in 1868, which deals with the word unit, and the second, composed shortly afterward, which treats Parmenides' 'great text' con-cerning Being and Not-Being.

A main theme in these papers is the opposition of the 'one and the many,' the problem that, following the Greeks, Hopkins views as central to realism. In the essay on Parmenides, he notes approvingly that Plato revered Parmenides as 'the great father of Realism.' Parmenides' asser-tion that 'Being is and Not-Being is not' is concerned with the problem of the multiplicity of things. In this essay, composed in the same year that he decided to become a priest, Hopkins made his first use of the terms *instress* and *inscape* in discussing Parmenides' idea of 'stress' as signifying Being, which holds things together and imparts reality to them. Parmenides evidently was germinal for his commitment to philo-sophical realism: 'But indeed I have often felt when I have ... felt the depth of an instress or how fast the inscape holds a thing that nothing is so pregnant and straightforward to the truth as simple *yes* and *is.*' With-out stress, Hopkins says, in part translating the Greek, 'There would be no ... stem of stress between us and things to bear us out and carry the mind over: without stress we might not and could not say / Blood is red / but only / This blood is red,' for then 'Universals would not be true' (J 127).

In 'The Position of Plato,' Hopkins presents the philosopher as transi-tional between the Sophists and Aristotle. He says that Plato felt 'the sadness of complex thought ... when the old unity of belief ... was gone'; in him we feel 'less his enthusiasm for the new truth [of Ideal Good] than his despair at the multiplicity of phenomena unexplained and unconnected,' since he must have recognized the 'incompatibilities' in 'his own ideals' (J 116). In 'Future of Metaphysics,' the poet integrates Plato into the first of 'three great seasons in the history of philosophy.' The first, 'led by the ideas Form and Matter,' is 'that of Plato, Aristotle, and the Schoolmen,' which 'at its most material' is 'still half metaphysical and abstract.' The second, led by 'Facts and Law,' is that of 'Bacon and physical science and Positivism,' whose 'most formal expressions are half physical and concrete.' The third is that of Hegel, which deals with historical development and 'must contradict itself whether it claims to be final or not.' The poet looks forward to a 'new Realism' that will 'challenge the prevalent philosophy of continuity or flux' (J 119–20). He speculates about the form this new realism will take, but it is clear that in 1867, at the end of his university studies, Hopkins is uncertain about the exact nature of the impending new version of realism, while he looks forward to it to counter the vogue of positivism. Duns Scotus, who, though medieval, was to satisfy the need he felt for a fresh approach, was still in his future.

The essay 'All words ...,' composed at same time as his composition on Parmenides, is especially suggestive for the development of Hopkins's concept of language and of poetry within the idealist-realist nexus. While the essay recognizes the force of convention in connecting sound with lexical sense, it also locates in the word unit complex implication beyond the arbitrary *signans-signatum* relationship. He distinguishes three 'terms' that belong to every 'word meaning a thing': first, 'its prepossession of feeling,' the affective impulse that precedes and motivates use of the word; second, 'its definition, abstraction, vocal expression or other utterance,' the word itself in its utterance; and third, 'its application ... the concrete things coming under it' in context. But 'in propriety' the word is found only in the 'middle term' and there only the expression, the *uttering* of the 'idea in the mind' (J 125). The poet's emphasis consistently is on the speaking – here a mental 'uttering'; the physical sounds effect the inner utterance. The internal 'uttering of the idea' fills the external form of the physical sounds. Applying this second 'term' to Hopkins's consistent emphasis on the oral performance of his poems, we infer that the first term, the 'prepossession' of the words, has first imparted to the physical sounds an affective significance. As the 'passion or enthusiasm' that motivates the utterance, it has a major importance for the development of Hopkins's idea of inscape and poeticlaness.

Hopkins's early essays show that the Greek idealist philosophers provided a major basis for his mature poetics that culminated in the 'Poetry and Verse' fragment, as well as for his formulation and practice of sprung rhythm. However, the poet's ideas were also significantly affected by the careful observation of the natural world that his journals reveal, which stimulated his abiding interest in the physical science of his day that Brown elucidates (187–326). The need to valorize sense experience in the frame of idealist thought probably explains the 'mercy from God' that he saw in his 1872 discovery of the writings of Duns Scotus, the early-fourteenth-century Franciscan, which made him 'flush with a new stroke of enthusiasm.' Afterwards, he reports, 'when I took in any inscape of the sky or sea I thought of Scotus' (J 221). Hopkins's idea of inscape originated not with Scotus, but rather with the poet's general realist convictions; nonetheless, he came to identify the concept with the Franciscan.

His partiality to Scotus, which 'became a passion,' was a rare thing in the nineteenth century. In his diary (1874), he tells of making 'the acquaintance of two and I suppose the only two Scotists in England in one week' (J 249). His preference for Scotus's version of realism over that of Thomas Aquinas, the version officially emphasized by the Jesuits, evidently cost him a final year of advanced study; a contemporary Jesuit commented confidentially to another Jesuit: '"He was too Scotist for his examiners"' (Roberts 70; see also White 284). As an 1875 letter to Bridges testifies, his enthusiasm for Scotus nevertheless endured. He reports having regretfully just put aside Aristotle's *Metaphysics*, presumably to concentrate on less secular matters, but he consoles himself that he can 'at all events ... read Duns Scotus and I care for him more even than Aristotle and more *pace tua* than a dozen Hegels' (LI 31). In the light of Jowett's and Green's interest in the German idealists, the comment on Hegel is another notable manifestation of Hopkins's intellectual independence. White is no doubt mistaken in thinking that the probing and philosophical Hopkins was simply ignorant of Hegel (White 100 and passim).

Telling poetic evidence of the poet's passion for the medieval Fransciscan and his realism is the fine sonnet *Duns Scotus's Oxford*, composed in 1879, which identifies Scotus as the one 'who of all men most sways my spirits to peace' (line 11). In the concluding tercet, prior to the final line that alludes to Scotus's famous argument for Mary's Immaculate Conception, 'Mary without spot,' the poem focuses on his *realism* ('realty'), identifying him as

> Of realty the rarest-veinèd unraveller; a not
> Rivalled insight, be rival Italy or Greece.   (12–13)

Time did not diminish Hopkins's interest in the 'Subtle Doctor.' In 1885, only four years before his death, he was corresponding with a friend about Scotus's reputed connection with Oxford (P 400).

Hopkins could have found in America a third Scotist to join his two English colleagues: the philosopher, scientist, and originator of 'pragmatism' and 'semiotics,' Charles Sanders Peirce (1839–1914), whose semiotics I have discussed and who, like the poet, resolved the problem of the particular and the general under Scotus's banner. In recent years Peirce has become widely, if not universally, recognized as 'the greatest philosopher the United States has ever seen' (Brent xiv). Like Hopkins, Peirce was deeply schooled in the idealist-realist tradition, and also – but as a professional scientist and philosopher – Peirce's investigations confirmed in him a strong belief in the integrity of physical phenomena, which led him first to nominalism but eventually to realism; Scotus's reasoning provided him with appropriately subtle solutions to the problem of the one and the many. And much like Hopkins, Peirce was led to declare himself a 'Scotistic realist.' In his semiotics physical fact or 'secondness' – the arena of nominalism – has a crucial place. But the generality of thirdness seeks to include the individuality of secondness, so that the problem of the validity of realism, found in language in 'words which represent things,' comes to the fore. Peirce's admiration for Scotus's version of realism shows up full force in his 1871 review of *Fraser's Berkeley* (1992, 88).

In analysing Scotus's thought, Louis Mackey says that in the 'Franciscan view' of realism, which Duns Scotus most thoroughly enunciates, 'the universal achieves full reality (concreteness) only in the singular, and the singular is only fully individuated (fully determinate) insofar as it is replete with universals' (147). As Mackey emphasizes, Scotus's idea is that one does not choose between universal and singular, as many realists as well as nominalists believe, but that they require each other – a conclusion that in its reconciliation of idealism with the material eminently suited both the English poet and Peirce.

Peirce's concept of the icon is compatible with his realism; the meaning of the icon's mental picture has an authentic, if not exact, relation to an underlying reality. In considering the development through time of word meaning, it is relevant that some well-known analysts have observed that for the native user symbolic language sound with repeated usage assumes a natural relationship with language meaning; that is to say, for the native user words become sound icons over time, and the arbitrariness of the symbolic significance fades. To hold that the arbitrary meaning assigned to the language symbol (*langue*) continues to be arbitrary implies that habits of usage simply deceive naïve users into thinking that the relationship is natural. Numerous theorists of language in the early and middle twentieth century took note of the problem that the implication of user naïveté raises. Roman Jakobson was among these theorists. In discussing the problem he cites particularly the 'timely' assertion of Émile Benveniste in a 1939 essay on the nature of linguistic signs, where, instead of positing the native user's naïveté, he finds 'crucial' the 'fact that only for a detached, alien onlooker is the bond between signans and signatum a mere contingence' (1971, 348); that is to say, habits of usage forge a stronger bond between sound and object with all language users; the sounds of 'hand' become a sound picture, a hieroglyph, of a hand. Dwight Bolinger makes much the same point in a chapter whose title declares, 'The Sign Is Not Arbitrary': 'an "arbitrary" form, once integrated into the [language] system, assumes all the *affective* and associative privileges enjoyed by the most obvious onomatopoeia' (1965, 231; my emphasis). In Peircean terms the symbolic in important ways becomes iconic.

We may apply similar ideas about the effect of habitual usage to Hopkins's analysis of word meaning in the essay, 'All words ...' In that context especially, Bolinger's 'affective' is an important adjective. For his native user, the word-sound carries a characteristic affect, 'feeling,' while in Hopkins's essay, the 'prepossession of the word' is explicitly its 'prepossession of *feeling*' (my emphasis). The feeling, affect, of a word also is comparable to Peirce's 'feeling' that is attached to the thought-sign. Hopkins says that a word has a 'passion or prepossession or enthusiasm which it has the power of suggesting, but not always or in everyone.' Benveniste's 'alien onlookers' – non-native speakers of the language – would be typical of those for whom the word does not evoke the prepossession; that is, the 'passion.' For them the connection between word and object indeed may be wholly arbitrary because they have not developed the feeling that makes the connection habitual in the language in question. In Hopkins's analysis, the spoken word not only 'suggests' the prepossession, but furthermore the prepossession is a property of the word, being 'in fact its *form.*' Manifestly, it is an underlying form that bears 'a valuable analogy to the soul' (J 125; my emphasis).

In the time between the essays 'All words ...' and 'Parmenides,' apparently a matter of only days or weeks, there is a significant development in Hopkins's metaphysical terminology. In his extant writings, the term *prepossession* occurs solely in the 'All words ...' essay of 1868. But prepossession seems to have a pair of more potent successors in *instress* and *inscape*, introduced in the 'Parmenides' essay. These words appear regularly thereafter in his diary entries, correspondence, and essays. However, unlike prepossession, which he applies only to spoken words, he attaches these terms to all kinds of sensory phenomena. He says inscape is 'design, pattern' (LI 66), and his usage indicates that instress is the force that vitalizes the inscape for the perceiver. The *Oxford English Dictionary* usefully defines it as 'the force or energy which sustains an inscape' (1989); instress leads to and supports inscape.

Consistent with the prepossession of a word being explicitly 'of feeling,' the association of inscape with affect becomes manifest in his diaries. In one entry, the poet describes the colour of the Lake of Brienz as 'the richest opaque green modulated with *an emotional instress* to blue' (J 176 [July 1868]); my emphasis), and he reports that when he viewed a comet, 'I felt a certain awe and instress, a feeling of strangeness' (249 [July 1874]). Instress generates perception of inscape. Thus, when in December 1872 the poet was 'on the fells with Mr. Lucas,' he reports seeing the 'inscape ... freshly, as if my eye were still growing, though with a companion [here, Lucas] the eye and the ear are for the most part shut and instress cannot come' (J 228). The 'growing' eye and the solitude usually required especially indicate that he is describing an inward, emotional experience. Indeed, the binding of instress and inscape to feeling appears from his first use of the terms when he speaks of Parmenides' 'feeling for instress ... and for inscape' and connects it with his own feeling, his sensory or emotional experience of 'Being.'

Hopkins had presented the 'passion or prepossession' as developing *over time*: the prepossession of the word 'evolves in the man and secondly in man historically.' The 'evolving' suggests, contrary to Christopher Devlin's otherwise compelling assertion that prepossession represents 'some remnant of the original power that first matched [the word] with reality' (Devlin 115), that it is rather the feeling that lies behind the word at the particular time of its usage. A word's prepossession follows its temporal development. Charles Peirce, in speaking of words as living, developing signs, finds a similar progression in word usage, instancing the continuing evolution of the meaning of electricity: 'Does not electricity mean more now than it did in the days of Franklin?' As the concepts that underlie words grow, lexical items like electricity come to mean more to users, not only in denotation but we may infer in connotative feeling. Over time, Peirce notes, it develops both 'in man and in the man.' Over centuries, we may understand, word meaning develops 'in man'; over a lifetime it develops 'in *the* man' (Peirce 1992, 54; see Weinsheimer 1991, 404–5).

The idea of the developing or 'evolving' word fits with the realism that both the poet and the semiotician-philosopher professed. For Hopkins the prepossession of the word is a passion that evolves 'connotatively' in the man. Peirce's view of a word's development is comparable to his description of the development of a 'theory' that progresses 'from a sign of a real object with which it is *acquainted*, passing from this, as its *matter*, to successive interpretants involving more and more fully its *form*, wishing ultimately to reach a direct perception of the entelechy' (1992, 304; his emphases). His concept of the word sign allows for incorporating in the word the feeling that develops 'connotatively' along with the developing abstract meaning. For the two Scotistic realists, Peirce and Hopkins, the evolution of word concepts over time is guided by underlying reality.

In 'All words ...' Hopkins describes works of art as comparable to individual words: 'Works of art of course like words utter the idea and in representing *real* things convey the prepossession with more or less success' (my emphasis). He characterizes the organization of the art work as a 'synthesis of ... impressions which gives us the unity with the prepossession conveyed by it,' thus associating it with the philosophically real. His ensuing description evokes the complex phonic organization of the meter, stress, intonation, and segmental sounds of one of his sprung rhythm poems: 'The further in anything, as a work of art, the organization is carried out, the deeper the form penetrates, the prepossession flushes the matter, the more effort will be required in apprehension, the more power of comparison, the more capacity for receiving that synthesis of ... impressions which gives us the unity with the prepossession conveyed by it' (J 126). Like Hopkins's association of the prepossession of the word with the work of art, Peircean semiotics finds that the two represent quite similar icons. John Sheriff, describing Peirce's concept of art as icon, could be speaking of Hopkins's idea of art in explaining that for Peirce the work of art consists in icons of feeling and quality: art 'presents us with *signs* of immediate consciousness, that is, feelings, qualities ... The *experience* of art as art, including literature despite its complex and often profound use of symbolic language, is primarily one of qualities and feelings rather than propositions and arguments' (78). Icons, rather than symbols, are the stuff of art and especially of lyric poetry.

While Hopkins's introduction of the word *inscape*, which he applies to all material phenomena including spoken words, antedates his discovery of Duns Scotus, Scotus enriched and valorized the term for him. In elucidating Scotus's concept of haecceity, the *thisness* of individual phenomena, Louis Mackey cites Hopkins's diary entry telling of his discovery of the Franciscan's work, where he says that afterward, 'when I took in any inscape of the sky or sea I thought of Scotus' (J 221). Mackey comments: 'The "inscape" that Hopkins speaks of is (loosely) the network of forms that you see when you look into a thing through its haecceity. That was what Scotus enabled Hopkins to see. For Scotus insists on the full reality and intelligibility of the individual, the reality of the formalities discerned in things by the mind, and the unity of the individual with the metaphysical tracery that composes it. One of the conditions of essential poetry is that universal and singular be interlinked, so that the unique can be represented in the general and the general manifested in the unique' (179). Mackey's analysis here of inscape and its implications suits very well what we know of Hopkins's education and philosophical convictions and can infer from his use of 'inscape' in his diaries and other writings.

Inscape is the scape of the set of formalities, the real generals – roughly, the universal principles – that lie behind each sensory phenomenon. Brown comes close to this position in calling 'inscape ... a "burl of being" or instress manifest in perceptible shapes,' instancing Hopkins's perception of an Alpine glacier as '"swerved and inscaped strictly to the motion of the mass"' or a waterfall as '"inscaped in fretted falling vandykes"' (231). Despite the intense interest in haecceity, sheer individuality, that such statements of Hopkins show, they do not abridge his commitment to the universal; rather, they illustrate it. The glacier and the waterfall reveal the physical laws of the 'motion of the mass.' As it was for Scotus, for Hopkins the particular and the general require each other. Of course, his usage reveals important differences between the inscapes of waterfalls and waves and the physical patterns of poetry and other art. The natural phenomena reveal the generality of the 'laws' that control them, while the speech sound patterns of poetry and the designs of all art have 'emotional' inscapes; their inscapes represent principles that lie behind the affective nature of humankind. No scientists have successfully codified human feeling. Implicit in Hopkins's holding that the force of 'love' is the motivator of poetry is a belief that love takes part in the inscape of poetry. But defining love, as with most words that refer to human feeling – the province of poetic inscape – has proved notoriously difficult.

Hopkins develops a very lively lexicon for his realist metaphysics. In the piece on Parmenides he introduces several key terms: along with instress and inscape, his first, as well as his chief use of *flush* and *foredrawn*.

Parmenides, he says, has a striking 'feeling for instress, for the flush and foredrawn, and for inscape' (J 127). *Flush* refers to fullness, *foredrawn* to boundedness and determinateness. In Brown's words, '"flushness" highlights the fluid informing principle of Being, while "the foredrawn" focuses on the bounding definition in which such force draws together as a unity' (174).

Parmenides' 'great text,' says Hopkins, 'is that Being is and Not-being is not' (J 127), and he explains the tautology: 'The truth in thought is Being, stress, and each word is one way of acknowledging Being and each sentence by its copula (or its equivalent) the utterance and assertion of it' (J 129). Being is a dynamic, not a static, state. Hopkins's continual emphasis on the role of utterance points up the centrality of the principle of stress in his analysis of the word. Without the unifying stress in the utterance, word and idea lack coherence: 'Taking the Idea for a hand and the name [word] for its glove left behind, then although to handle it by the concrete may leave it a dry crumpled piece of skin, abstraction may as injuriously blow it out into a graceless bladdery animation' (quoted in Brown 160). The material word sounds of themselves are empty gloves; the abstract meanings of the words are formless bladders, lacking the structure that the glove imparts. The act of utterance animates the sounds, and its stress flushes and foredraws, fills and defines the rich iconic significance, manifesting its metaphysical reality. Hopkins thinks that poetry can reveal this significance, that it is inherent in the inscape of the word or the work of art and is made accessible to contemplation by the phonetic repetitions of artful but natural utterance, even as the reality of natural objects is made accessible to the contemplative observer in the veining of leaves and the forms of waves.

That words and works of art have prepossessions that *connote* the ultimate reality of their objects, as Hopkins's essay suggests, is certainly congenial with the realist position. The 'prepossession' – the term that in Hopkins's usage seems to be the predecessor of inscape – of the word or work of art is the form of the feeling, the passion or enthusiasm that the utterance of the material sounds manifests. Poets like Eliot and Frost, while implicitly agreeing that the material quality of speech sound carries a defining significance in poetical composition, do not attempt analysis of the phenomenon. Hopkins, characteristically explicit, does offer such analysis. In his scheme, as indicated in the essays 'All words ...' and 'Poetry and Verse,' the distinctive meanings of poetic language arise not principally from abstract lexical meanings, but from the feelings that precede and develop as word sounds. 'Feeling,' a defining aspect of Hopkins's concept of a 'prepossession of feeling,' provides a rationale for the affective complexities of the linguistic and poetic.

Hopkins fixes on verbal utterance, rather than rhetorical intricacies of discursive meaning, as that which manifests the special quality of poeticalness. Uttered speech sounds provide the scape, being the perceptible external representation of the prepossession or inscape of the word. This essence finally is available only to individual contemplation, 'in which the mind is absorbed ... taken up by, dwells upon, enjoys, a single thought.' 'In its absoluteness,' he states, such contemplation 'is impossible unless in a trance' (apparently a trance like that of religious mystics). For the most part, repetition of 'the same energy on the same matter' has to suffice (J 126). Hopkins's assertion of the efficacy of repetition of a single thought for achieving a contemplative state provides a precedent for his explanation of the value of verse repetition in 'Poetry and Verse' six years later, after his discovery of Duns Scotus and while he was developing sprung rhythm. As I have noted previously, he presents the repetitions of metre and rhyme as proper to verse, but not strictly necessary to poetry. Poetry detaches speech inscape, with verse repetitions, '*oftening, over-and-overing, aftering* of the inscape,' providing the usual instrument for effecting the detachment (J 289).

Hopkins came to this distinction between poetry and verse only after writing his undergraduate essays. Thus, in his very early Platonic dialogue, 'On the Origin of Beauty' (1865), he draws the conventional contrast between prose and poetry, the term *poetry* virtually predicating verse form. The Professor, the voice of authority in the piece, summarizes: 'If therefore by poetry you understand all verse, we may define it as differing from prose in having a continuous and regular artificial structure ... if by poetry you mean only noble verse, then let us define verse as above, and merely add that poetry is a particular case of it, namely the case of its being noble and successful' (J 107). Hopkins at that point had not yet developed his notion of the centrality of speech utterance and its inscape to poetry. By the time he wrote 'Poetry and Verse,' however, he had adopted the idea that the inscape of the speech-sound figure defines the poetical. The distinction is now between poetry and verse, not between 'noble and successful' verse on the one hand, and prose on the other. Poetry for Hopkins came to signify a quality of verbal composition.

But how does one recognize poeticalness, inscape, in the speech-sound figure? Hopkins is quite ready to assert its presence or non-presence, using it as a criterion in many of his statements about poetry and art. However, he never analyses the speech-sound figures of a specific poem or even one such figure. He tells Bridges that inscape is 'design, pattern' (LI 66), thus suggesting that one should look for it in the shape or 'scape' of the sounds. But the patterns of inscape exist in the world of forms (formalities), and what the shape of a sound figure is in that world seems highly problematical.

As a realist concept inscape is closely implicated in the central problem of realism of the one and the many, the one common nature and its many manifestations. Christopher Devlin's exposition of Duns Scotus's solution to the problem perhaps clarifies the thinking of the poet, professedly a Scotistic realist. Scotus, says Devlin, erased the opposition in Aristotle's dictum that 'Intellect deals with universal ideas, sense with particular things' and saw the two faculties as covering the same field. Thus, 'sensation responds to a real object outside the mind,' yet the object strikes independently on *sense* and *intellect*, the latter coming first (121). Intellect apprehends first an object's general nature – we might instance the nature of the rhythmic foot – and it then perceives the particular sensory forms as instances of the foot.

In the process, according to Scotus, one's perception follows an evolutionary process that reveals the *species specialissima*, the most particular form with its special combination of formalities, which is the 'dynamic image of nature being created' (Devlin 196). We may 'be momentarily aware of nature evolving as a pattern of sense-qualities in the very instant that we are aware of the individual ... but *before* abstraction has taken place which would isolate the individual from the pattern.' The *species specialissma*, Devlin speculates, is a close Scotistic equivalent to inscape. This interpretation of inscape suggests a refinement of Mackey's conclusion that inscape is the 'network' of formalities that one sees through an individual entity's 'thisness.' Taking man as an instance, Devlin says that the *species specialissima* of man is not any particular person, but rather the 'Ideal Person to whom universal nature tends' (196), essentially man before the Fall; that is, before sense and intellect were divided. This ideal person would incorporate, then, the formalities that form ideal man before individuation. Devlin cites as apposite (200) the 'Argument' that prefaces Hopkins's sonnet, *Henry Purcell*: 'The poet wishes well to the divine genius of Purcell and praises him that, whereas other musicians have given utterance to the moods of man's mind, he has, beyond that, uttered in notes the very make and species of man as created both *in him* and *in man generally*' (P 157; my emphases). In his music Purcell 'uttered in notes' both the individual and the general images of man. The *species specialissima* makes the two images perceptible simultaneously, though fleetingly, and so, suggests Devlin, does *inscape*. This is not to suggest that Scotus finds that unfallen Adam was not individuated, but instead that the *species specialissima* is the ideal person before individuation. The statement in the 'Argument' about Purcell's musical composition is particularly suggestive for Hopkins's idea of poetic inscape, since patterned sound is the material of both poetic verse and music.

Devlin also finds apposite to Scotus's *species specialissima* the individual entity in the process of being created, the description in the last lines of Hopkins's curtal sonnet *Ashboughs*, which envisions 'old earth's groping towards the steep / Heaven whom she child's us by.' 'Old earth,' Devlin says, is the common nature, 'the *Natura Communis* which in each man is a principle formally distinct from his individuality' or haecceity (195). Heaven's special impregnation supplies Scotistic haecceity, which 'might be called in modern terms bare particularity' (Mackey 173). The Creator finally stamps each created person with individuality, and at the same time each person possesses its traits, its formalities, that are common to humans. Recognition of its individuality and its shared formalities, as in a work of art, can impart an experience of inscape, inscape being for Hopkins what 'above all I aim at in poetry' (LI 66). In the case of appreciation of poetic verse, then, concentration on the common features in the rich phonetic, contextual, and historical individuality of the verse utterance can lead to the experience.

In his student essay on Parmenides, Hopkins cites with tacit approval the ontological equation, 'To be and to know or Being and thought are the same' (129). The created world, held together by Being, provides thought with access to the real nature of things. By means of 'contemplation,' a person concentrating on 'a single thought' insofar as possible (J 125–6) can 'catch' an instress of the inscape, the underlying general form of an existent object, at the same time as the person catches its individuality. Such insight seems to have been Hopkins's ultimate purpose in his own minute observations and descriptions of the phenomena of nature. He aims to experience, by means of an instress, the inscape that lies behind or within the scapes of God's fascinating creation.

'Parmenides' and the 'All words ...' essays are important in the background of the 'Poetry and Verse' fragment, Hopkins's most definitive statement of the nature of poetry. They indicate how the early Greeks led Hopkins to his eventual understanding that the spoken sound of language is the conveyor of its poetical element that he terms its inscape. He comes to a belief that speech sound conveys 'connotatively' the sense experience behind and beyond the abstract lexical content. One gathers that each of the sound figures of spoken language – whether rhythm, letters, words, or sentences – have significant affective content that produces characteristic feelings. Contemplation of the sound scapes, seen through their 'thisness,' may lead to insight into their inscape, which we may think involves the individual and collective history of the poetic words, of their sounds and of their meanings. The auditory experience of a speech-sound figure potentially is comparable to the visual experience that Hopkins describes in viewing an arch of a castle ruin: 'standing before the gateway I had an instress which only the true old work gives from the strong and noble inscape of the pointed arch' (J 263 [1875]). The arch does not produce the instress by virtue of its shape and materials alone. The experience requires the context of the 'true old work,' including its complex architectural background. The inscape of the sound figures of a poem similarly implicates all of their linguistic history, notably the affective aspects.

Hopkins's theories of language and poetry underwent important changes between his early university days and his late twenties. His thinking perhaps was stimulated by his teaching of rhetoric at Roehampton in 1873–4 when he was twenty-nine. At about that time speech sound came to the fore in his formulations both of sprung rhythm and of language inscape. In Hopkins' early diary entries (1863–4), the numerous lists of phonetically and etymologically related words are of interest for the development of his techniques of alliteration and *skothending*, but they have no direct relevance to his later ideas about poetical language. At one early point he suggests that particular sounds are related to a particular range of lexical meaning; *crack*, *creak*, and *crackle*, he states, 'must be onomatopoetic' (J 5). But onomatopoetic evocation of lexical meanings is not instrumental in detaching poetic inscape, which is a matter of feeling, not word meaning. Poetry for Hopkins foregrounds the sensory and emotional inscape, particularly aided by verse's repetitions of the speech-sound figures.

Hopkins presents his theory as applicable to poetry in general, but for purposes of example the repetitions of sound figures in his own works provide excellent illustrative prototypes. The octave of the sonnet *Duns Scotus's Oxford* is a typical and successful example of sprung rhythm. (In the following passage italics represent the 'outrides' that the poet indicates. To point up the repetitions, I underline the alliterations on the stresses, and use acute accents to mark all the stresses, six of which the poet specifies.)

T̲ówery cíty and bránchy be̲twéen t̲ówers;
Cuckoo-écho*ing*, bell swár*mèd*, lark-chár*mèd*, rook-r̲ácked, river-r̲óunded;
The dápple-eared l̲íly be̲lów *thee*; that cóuntry and tówn did
Ónce en̲cóun*ter in*, here c̲óped and p̲óisèd p̲ówers;

Thou hást a b̲áse and b̲ráckish s̲kírt there, s̲óurs
That n̲éighbor-n̲áture thy g̲réy béauty is g̲róunded
Bést in; g̲ráceless g̲rówth, thou hást confóunded
R̲úral r̲ural kéep*ing* – f̲ólk, f̲lócks, and f̲lówers.

Metrical repetition pervades the passage. There are two uniform stanzas
of four lines, each line having five feet built around the stresses and the
same rhyme pattern. Segmental repetition, lettering, is powerful. Each
of two rhyme sounds occurs four times, twenty-six of the forty stressed
syllables alliterate with at least one other in the same line. Furthermore,
the two rhyme sounds, -*ours*, and -*ounded*, share the -*ow* sound. There are
also important repetitions outside the metrical patterns and the lettering: the rhythmic pattern of the compounds in the second line, the past
participial -*d*s and -*èd*s throughout, the complex phonetic echoes in lines
6 and 7 of g̲r̲e̲y̲ and g̲r̲aceless, g̲r̲ounded and g̲r̲ow̲t̲h̲; alliteration on
secondary stresses, and the whole-word repetitions of *tower-* and *rural*.

This is to inventory partially the repetitions in the sound scape of the
passage. We might talk about the effects of the sounds in the manner of
Mallarmé's observation that, contrary to their meanings, the front vowel
of *nuit* sounds light, while the back vowel of *jour* sounds dark, and assert
that the repetitions of the back diphthong -*ow* lend a darkness to the
Duns Scotus octave. But it is difficult to understand how one goes from
such statements about the scape to insight into the inscape, from the
physical sounds and their sensory and emotional implications to an
experience of their inner charge. In his comments on his own poetry or
the poetry of others, as I have said, Hopkins provides no model for such
analysis. One may assume that one gets from a scape to an inscape
through a process of contemplation, repeating 'the same energy on the
same matter' (J 126), which contrasts with the 'transitional' processes of
reason (J 125–6). But it is not possible to explain something non-rational
using language, whose processes characteristically rely on reason.

Perhaps more promising than trying to explain the mental process of
getting from scape to inscape is another aspect of Mallarmé's observation, the synaesthetic nature of his relating an aural perception to a
visual experience, that is, objecting to the use of a back vowel sound to

denote an experience of brightness. In terms of philosophical realism, it may suggest that a 'real general,' a common principle, lies behind experiencing physical sound as light. Hopkins had a lively synaesthetic sense that he applied, for example, in his statement to Bridges, quoted earlier, about the 'charm' of the 'Westcountry instress' of Barnes's poetry. He associates the verse variously with certain traditional songs, the poetry of Herbert and Herrick, certain landscapes of western England, and smells of wildflowers and apples (LI 88). In Scotistic terms, we may infer that the inscape, the real generals or 'formalities,' peculiar to Barnes's Dorsetshire can be expressed in terms of hearing, sight, and smell, though it is based, first of all, in the speech-sound figures.

Hopkins asserts that successful art by means of its patterns produces an instress, revealing true inscape. When he tells Bridges that 'feeling, love in particular is the great moving power of verse' (LI 66), one gathers that feeling characterizes the inscape of successful poetry. In the same letter to Bridges he correlates inscape in poetry with music and painting: 'as air, melody, is what strikes me most of all in music and design in painting, so design, pattern or what I am in the habit of calling "inscape" is what above all aim at in poetry' (LI 66). We infer that he has in mind the pattern revelatory of inner, metaphysical structure and motion, as with the glacier, referred to above, that Hopkins describes as 'swerved and inscaped' by its movement (quoted in Brown 231). However, he does not go beyond such general remarks to analyse poetic speech sound figures that lead to instresses. For lack of such poetic analysis, it may be productive to consider some of the poet's later journal entries that do analyse particular paintings in terms of inscape.

Hopkins devoted several journal pages to commenting on paintings in the 1874 exhibition at the Academy in London, often remarking on the presence and absence of instress and inscape. As a practised amateur artist, the brother of two professionals, and a bold, inveterate theorist, he judges with some confidence. Commenting on one Millais painting, he finds that an instress is lacking: 'Millais – *Scotch Firs: "The silence that is in the lonely woods"* – No such thing, instress absent, firtrunks ungrouped, four or so pairing but not markedly, true bold realism but quite a casual install of woodland with casual heathertufts.' The synaesthetic portrayal of silence that the epigraph asserts, then, is not borne out. So too, as he continues, he finds another Millais painting lacking the emotional instress of the declining season that its title asserts: '*Winter Fuel: "Bare ruined choirs"* etc – almost no sorrow of autumn' (J 244). Yet he sometimes finds that a work that does not produce an instress still has valuable qualities, for example, an engraving of Lawrence Alma-Tadema's painting *Vintage Festival*. He reports that it 'impressed the thought one would gather also from Rembrandt in some measure and from many great painters less than Rembrandt / of a master of scaping rather than of inscape. For vigorous rhetorical but realistic and unaffected scaping holds everything but no arch-inscape is thought of' (J 245). Or he may find that the contrary is true: an art work may reveal inscape but be defective in rhetoric, as he finds Wordsworth's poetry weak in rhetoric (LII 141), but at the same time sees in certain of Wordsworth's apparently 'simple pieces ... a subtle complexity of emotion' (J 112), affective riches that produce an instress. In direct contrast to Wordsworth's poetry, then, the painting of Alma-Tadema shows a mastery of rhetoric but provides no access to inscape. The artist's rhetoric supplies vigour and naturalness to the 'scape.' Inscape provides something beyond; it constitutes the peculiar element of true art, whether painting, poetry, architecture, or music.

One extensive commentary analyses a Millais painting entitled *Daydream* that Hopkins thoroughly admires. In accord with his definition of the poetic as residing in the inscape of speech-sound figures, the commentary on this work begins with matters of design, colour, disposition of shapes, textures, and such. He calls *Daydream* 'a Millais-Gainsborough most striking crossbreed; colouring raw, blue handkerchief not any stuff in particular but Reynolds' emphatic *drapery*, background (bushes and tank) either unfinished or mere mud.' As he proceeds, he finds in the representation of the daydreamer's face features that directly reveal inscape: 'Intense expression of character, not mood, true inscape – I think it could hardly be exceeded. Features long, keeling, and Basque. The fall away of the cheek (it is a 3/4 face) masterly.' This statement seems at variance with his poetic theory, by which the poetical resides in repeating speech-sound figures that are 'over and above meaning,' The commentary that follows gets back to matters of design: 'Great art in the slighted detail of the hat on the lap, blue of the bracelet, lace of scarf; fingers resting on or against one another very true and original (see on Holman Hunt's *Shadow of Death* much the same thing)' (J 245).

The poet's analyses of the Academy exhibition indicate that his aesthetic canons for visual art differ from his tenets for poetry and, for that matter, for music. Finding inscape in the presentation of the dreamer's face, which Hopkins sees as showing permanent character rather than passing mood, seems perfectly consistent with the idea that inscape is found in presentation of real generals, common natures, in specific individuals. But the inscape of poetry in his theory resides in the nonrepresentational sound figures. The difference in the standards evidently lies in the physical media; poetry's images are symbolic, mediated by arbitrary word sounds, while painting's pictures are direct representations.

The emphasis that he places in his early theoretical writings on the effects of repetition and parallelism in art generally, as well as the importance accorded to the role of repetition of the speech-sound figure in 'Poetry and Verse,' also is not reflected in his commentary on the paintings. His discussion of art in the essay 'On the Origin of Beauty' (J 87–95), written years before (1865), deals at length with the matter of symmetry and dissymmetry, an aspect of art closely involved with parallelism and repetition. In 'Poetic Diction,' a piece written near the same time, he asserts categorically, 'The artificial part of poetry, *perhaps we shall be right to say all artifice*, reduces itself to the principle of parallelism' (J 84; my emphasis).

In sprung rhythm, 'stress *is* the life,' and it is the dominating element of repetition in the feet and lines. Hopkins also fostered repetitive effect by quantitatively equalizing the feet, the equalization becoming especially apparent in the poet's practice of repeating foot patterns within lines. The second line of *Duns Scotus's Oxford* provides a remarkable example of the impact that the poet typically works for: 'Cuckoo-écho*ing*, bell-swárm*èd*, lark-chárm*èd*, rook-rácked, river-róunded.' The parallel spondaic quality (disregarding the outrides) of the five feet is striking. Because of the rhymes with 'river-róunded,' I assign primary stress to the first syllables of the participles. A more accurate analysis probably would be to assign divided stress to all the feet: 'Cùckoo écho*ing*, bèll-swárm*èd*.'

The poet's aim to effect detachment of a speech figure through repetition of phonetic pattern seems as manifest in this line as in any other line of his poetry. Just as he found in Barnes's poetry a 'Westcountry instress' comparable to that produced by certain wildflowers and folk tunes, so we might posit that by means of weighty compounding, Hopkins strives for an 'English' instress. His comment on Barnes's theory of the English language shows that along with his poetry he admired the other's embrace of Old English as representing the basic character of the native language. In recommending Barnes to Bridges, he couches approval of his poetic techniques and his writings on Anglo-Saxon in a commentary on the impracticality of his aspirations for the modern language:

Talking of chronologically impossible and long words the Rev. Wm. Barnes, good soul, of Dorset-dialect poems (in which there is more true poetry than in Burns) has published a 'Speech craft of English speech' = English Grammar, written in an unknown tongue, a sort of modern Anglosaxon, beyond all that Furnival in his wildest Forewords ever dreamed. He does not see the utter hopelessness of the thing. It makes one weep to think what English might have been; for in spite of all that Shakspere and Milton have done with the compound I cannot doubt that no beauty in a language can make up for want of purity. In fact I am learning Anglo-Saxon and it is a vastly superior thing to what we have now. But the madness of an almost unknown man trying to do what the three estates of the realm together could never accomplish! He calls degrees of comparision pitches of suchness: we *ought* to call them so, but alas! (LI 163)

One gathers from Barnes's writings on language that he favoured composing poetry in the Dorset dialect in part because he saw it as representing an earlier and therefore purer state of English, less diluted by Norman French and Latin and naturally more conservative than London English. He wrote extensively about Anglo-Saxon, including the *An Outline of English Speechcraft,* which Hopkins refers to here, and an elementary grammar; in the process he tried to revive the older language, which all the king's men 'could never accomplish.'

Despite his patronizing tone here, Hopkins was sincerely in sympathy with Barnes's attempt. Like him, he admired in the sounds of the earlier language the preponderance of closed syllables and strong consonants and in the verse system the heavy stressing and alliteration. Both poets saw Anglo-Saxon, with its minimal mongrelization from the French, as embodying more fully the distinctive English character and the deep feeling characteristic of its inscape. Nevertheless, it was not from a chauvinistic belief in a natural superiority of elemental Englishness over the endowments of other languages that Hopkins laments the decline of Old English from its former state. Instead, his disappointment arises from a feeling that its spoken sounds share in the natural constitution of his homeland. He probably wanted his line of five strong compounds, along with other less obvious sound figures, such as the native suffixes – -*ish* ('brickish') and -*y* ('towery,' 'branchy'), to impart a basic Englishness to the inscape of the octave. At the same time, he presumably would likewise applaud Pindar's work for its Greek qualities.

It also would not be true to Hopkins's Scotistic realism to think that he attributed to Barnes's verse a nebulous 'Westcountry spirit' like no other, or that he strove to evoke in his own work an Englishness unrelated to other peoples and places. We might rather think of such regional traits in terms of shared formalities. The type 'man,' a Scotist might tell us, is constituted of a great number of formalities natural to the species. But human beings of one community or another may typically share in common a distinctive set of formalities, apparent to some extent in common traits of their fellow citizens and of the country-side, which other national types possess in different combinations. In each separate being the combination of formalities is quite apart from its individuality, haecceity; the particular admixture of formalities in human beings mainly accounts for national and regional characters and differences.

That Hopkins saw people as in the first place belonging to a single, undivided, and overarching species is made explicit in his poem *Henry Purcell*, composed in April 1879, a month after *Duns Scotus's Oxford*. The works clearly make a pair in that each is a sprung rhythm long-line sonnet heavy in outriding syllables that celebrates a creative genius of England's past whose works made him very dear to the poet. The prose argument and the poetic subject matter of the Purcell poem centre on the composer's having 'uttered in notes the very make and species of man,' as the argument puts it in terms evocative of Duns Scotus' realism. In a letter to Bridges, Hopkins with uncharacteristic vehemence denies that there are subjective – nominalistic – implications in his words: 'My sonnet means "Purcell's music is none of your d—d subjective rot"' (LI 84). No dry philosophical concept, realism for the poet was a subject for passionate partisanship. In the poem proper, Hopkins expresses the overriding significance of Purcell's presentation of the inscape of hu-man nature, its 'forgèd feature' (stress marks are Hopkins's; italics signals outrides):

> Not mood in him nor mean*ing*, proud fire or sacred fear,
> Or love, or pity, or all *that* sweet notes not his might nursle;
> It is the forgèd feature finds me; it is the rehearsal
> Of own, abrúpt sélf *there* so thrusts *on*, so thróngs the éar.

'Forgèd feature' and 'abrúpt sélf' here, as the argument confirms, refer to the universal selfhood of mankind, whose inscape Purcell's work evokes, rather than to Purcell's individual self.

The composer achieves his 'utterance' of humankind's common na-ture by musical means, presumably by music that is in harmony with man's nature. It is notable that Hopkins's tenets for music have much more in common with those he holds for poetry than do his canons for painting, which differ notably from them. In his notes on 'Rhythm' in verse, as quoted in chapter 2, above, he presents music, like verse, as a 'recasting' of speech. 'The musical syllable is the note, the musical foot or word the bar,' and so on, proceeding right down to 'the movement for the paragraph, the piece for the discourse' (J 273). Hopkins sees the human voice as the arch-musical instrument and musical grammar as being like that of language. Furthermore, musical composition is like verse in its artful repetition: as poetry is 'speech wholly or partially repeating some kind of figure which is over and above meaning,' so 'Music is composition which wholly or partially repeats the same figure of pitched sound (it is the aftering of pitched sound).' The notable difference is that 'Some matter and meaning is essential [to verse] but only as an element necessary to support and employ the shape which is contemplated for its own sake' (J 289–90). The analogy to music that Hopkins draws indicates that the pattern of poetry's rhythms and word-sounds can produce inscapes like Purcell's compositions. Hopkins even suggests to his brother Everard that, 'perhaps the inflections and intonations of the speaking voice may give effects more beautiful than any attainable by the fixed pitches of music' (LIV 220).

Hopkins surely means in the grand speech music of the culminating sestet of the poem to evoke the inscape of Purcell's music, where he 'uttered in notes the very make and species of man' (italics signal outrides):

> Let him oh! With his air of an*gels* then lift me, lay *me*! only I'll
> Have an eye to the sakes *of him*, quaint moon*marks*, to his pelted plumage
>   under
> Wíngs; so some great storm*fowl*, whenever he has walked his while
> The thunder-purple seabeach, plumèd purple-of-thunder,
> If a wuthering of his pal*my* snow-pi*nions* scatter a colossal smile
> Off *him*, but meaning mo*tion* fans fresh our wits with wonder.   (9–14)

To note briefly some details of the repetitive pattern of 'lettering' here: In line 9, the manuscript signals an elision of 'only' with 'I'll,' which produces 'on*l*'I'll,' adding to the *l* alliterations, making in the six stresses three alliterations on vowels and three on *l* – all six being sonorants. The next four lines, while maintaining the sonority with numerous liquids and nasals, introduce also the 'bumpy music' of the voiceless stops, notably *p*: 'pelted plumage,' 'thunder-purple,' 'plumèd purple-of-thunder,' 'palmy snow-pinions.' The final line provides a grand culmination to the pattern of lettering, returning to the dominant sonority of the poem with seven nasals and three sets of alliterating labials, *m*, *w*, and *f*: 'but méaning mótion fans frésh our wíts with wónder.'

Through his sprung rhythm verse, Hopkins too 'throng[s] the ear' with work that variously expresses 'the very make and species of man,' but instead of Purcell's 'air of angels,' pitched music, he repetitively uses figures of speech sound, to which sprung rhythm is especially adapted. Clearly, the recurrence of the rhythmic units of both poet and composer can facilitate detachment of the inscape for 'contemplation of the mind.'

The process of contemplation that leads to perception of inscape, in which the mind is absorbed by a single thought, is disturbingly indescribable. Though Duns Scotus's theory of haecceity and formalities can lead to a viable proposal for the poet's concept of inscape, it does not and cannot lead to detailed analyses of individual cases. Man is comfortable with reasoning, the process 'in which one thought sensation follows another' (J 125); linguistic meanings usually result from such a process. But for man to perceive inscape, his contemplative sensibility must be opened. In expressing man's inscape, the poet suggests, Henry Purcell's music can lead the hearer to an 'instress,' but the music speaks in an untranslatable language of feeling.

At the same time, though language can't really deal with details of poetic inscape either, we can attempt to come closer to it by looking at the repetitive speech-sound scapes of the affective language that the poet plentifully employs. In the octave of *Duns Scotus's Oxford* we might cite the harsh *gr*s in the description of the discordant new brick buildings of Oxford: the structures sour 'that neighbour-nature thy grey beauty is grounded / Best in; graceless growth.' (6–7). But more pervasive in the poem, and more notable for the physical feeling attached to them, are the contrasting smooth 'liquid' consonants *l* and *r*, as in 'dapple-eared lily below thee' (3), and especially at the conclusion of the octave: 'Rural rural keeping – folk, flocks, and flowers' (8). This phonic theme culminates in the final tercet of the sonnet that celebrates Scotus as, 'Of realty the rarest veinèd unraveller; a not rivalled insight, be rival Italy or Greece' (12–13). The feeling inherent in the sound scapes echoes in the lexical contrast of the 'graceless' new buildings with the 'rural rural keeping' that Oxford is 'grounded best in.' This, of course, is to suggest mimetic features of the sound scape as they relate to the words, but the affective nature of the sounds may bear indirectly on the inscape.

A comparable density of liquid consonants continues in the two poems that Hopkins composed at virtually the same time as the Duns Scotus sonnet, *Binsey Poplars* and *Henry Purcell* (1879). More pointedly than *Duns Scotus's Oxford*, *Binsey Poplars* mourns the transformations of the Oxford scene. While the emphasis in the former is on the enduring natural beauty of Oxford in the frame of the Franciscan's triumphant achievement, *Binsey Poplars* focuses on nature and is elegiac in tone:

> My aspens dea̲r̲, whose ai̲r̲y cages que̲ll̲ed,
> Qué̲ll̲ed or quenched in l̲eaves the l̲eaping sun,
> A̲ll̲ fé̲ll̲ed, fé̲ll̲ed, are á̲ll̲ fé̲ll̲ed. (1–3)

The repetitions of the dominant liquids in 'quelled,' 'felled,' and 'all,' culminating in the repetition of 'rural' (similarly repeated in 'rural, rural keeping' in *Duns Scotus's Oxford* 8), abetted by the sibilant *ss*, contribute especially to producing an affective impact:

> S̲t̲r̲ókes of havoc úns̲e̲lve
>   The s̲weet es̲pecial s̲c̲ene,
> R̲ú̲r̲al s̲c̲ene, a r̲u̲r̲al s̲c̲ene,
> S̲wéet es̲pe̲c̲ial r̲u̲r̲al s̲c̲ene. (21–4)

'Especial scene' repeated, and 'rural scene' reiterated three times, unsubtly but effectively foreground the sounds.

Henry Purcell also shows this consonantal motif. Repetition of words dominated by liquids occupy the first line: 'Have fai̲r̲ fa̲ll̲en, O fai̲r̲, fai̲r̲ have fa̲ll̲en, so dea̲r̲'; and subsequently every rhyme word in the poem has one or more: 'dea̲r̲,' 'hea̲r̲,' 'Pu̲r̲ce̲ll̲,' 're̲ve̲r̲sa̲l̲,' and so on. And while the subject matter and emotional tone are quite different from the other two works, the comparable quality of the recurring sound scape may be thought similarly to conduce to an 'emotional instress.'

Hopkins's most intensive use of word repetition that overtly foregrounds the phonic effect is found throughout *The Leaden Echo and the Golden Echo*, quite markedly in the endings of the two sections, where liquid l̲ and r̲, nasal n̲ are dominant and then the glides y̲ and w̲ join these in importance. The *Leaden Echo* ends:

> Be beginning to despair, to despair,
> Despair, despair, despair, despair. (15–16)

And the *Golden Echo* section concludes:

Yónder. – What high as that! We follow, now we follow. – Yónder, yes yonder,
   yonder,
Yónder.   (47–8)

The synaesthetic term *liquid* that linguists apply to *l*s and *r*s is suggestive
of the sensory quality that the sounds of themselves impart to the phonic
scape of the poems and may be indicative of Scotistic formalities that
speech sounds share with other human and cosmic entities. But the
scape is not formed simply by the physical sounds, which of themselves
are 'dry ... crumpled skin.' According to Hopkins's concept of poetry,
the scaping, and a fortiori the inscaping, depend on the act of *uttering*
the words, which implicates the immediate phonic environment and a
full record of the affective content of the word sounds and meanings in
their customary contexts. Thus, repetition of words in the poems, combined with the neighbour words that relate to them phonically, carries
more consequential sound scapes than the letter sounds alone. 'Rural'
seems especially pregnant in the phrases in both the Duns Scotus poem,
'Rural rural keeping,' and in *Binsey Poplars*. Similarly affective, and effective, are the verbal sound repetitions in 'All felled, felled, are all felled,'
in *Binsey Poplars* and in 'Have fair fallen, O fair, fair have fallen' in *Henry
Purcell*.

A musical composition may have representational features, but they
will not be an essential aspect of the scape or the inscape that Hopkins
implies in stating that Purcell's music *utters* 'the very make and species of
man.' The phonic design of a sonata's or a sonnet's scape can animate
an instress of human inscape aside from such representation. In *Duns
Scotus's Oxford*, the poet celebrates the Franciscan's insight into 'realty,'
which is the domain of inscape, and at the same time brings out through
the poem's combination of *speech* sounds his own phonic version of
mankind's nature. In *Henry Purcell* realism is again central, in both its
subject and its form and in its praise of the 'forgèd feature' of Purcell's
music, which shows rather than explicates the *real* nature of mankind.
The poem evokes, through its use of highly wrought sprung rhythm
verse, the inscape of human speech sound – the 'network of forms' that
characterizes mankind's nature.

'Poetry and Verse' presents the poetical aspect of a composition as
manifesting the inscape of figures of speech sound. In that essay verse
form itself is accorded only the ancillary function of detaching the
inscape for contemplation by means of its repetitions; verse regularities
have no separate poetical function. But elsewhere, as in his letter to

Everard, he speaks of the 'symmetrical beauties of verse' (LIV 220), implicitly granting to verse a positive function beyond the force of repetition. In addition, in his various writings Hopkins continually discusses and emphasizes the centrality of stress in establishing the recurrent structural divisions, and he pays much attention to the role of metrical length in making the feet uniform. In his correspondence and his later verse compositions and annotations, he also recognizes a close relationship between the repeating sound patterns of verse and those of pitched music, whose aesthetic qualities clearly depend on its repetitive structure. Identifying music as a 'recasting of speech used in a wide sense,' he focuses on the regular divisions into 'uniform lengths and accentuations' (J 273). The comparison implies analogically that verse's 'symmetrical beauties' make a direct positive contribution to the inscape beyond their function of detaching it.

This chapter has attempted to explore the central concept of Hopkins's aesthetic perception, inscape, insofar as his writings warrant. His discussions of the term and his uses of it permit substantial insight into the idea behind it. But he himself does not apply the term to analysis of particular poems, and any attempt to explicate its workings in specific works seems doomed to fall short of a lucid explanation. This is inevitable. The concept is metaphysical, and so by definition it is based on speculative reasoning not confirmed by observation. Hopkins's theory nevertheless offers a stimulating response to the widespread observation that literature provides insight into otherwise hidden aspects of existence.

It is manifest that the poet was a highly imaginative person with an education in realism and idealism under teachers of the first order, along with a highly original, well-controlled facility for understanding and developing sophisticated theoretical concepts. Despite leaving an unavoidable vagueness in the specific application of inscape, he provides us with good evidence for certain basic assertions about it. First, his diaries and correspondence, especially, supply ample reason to take his commitment to Duns Scotus's realism in earnest and to look for inscape in the web of Scotus's formalities and haecceity. Secondly, one should not expect to find inscape directly in particular rhetorical techniques, particular use of sound patterns, or particular representations: these help to form the scape of a work of art, not the inscape; the inscape lies behind.

Thirdly, despite the distinction between scape and inscape, it can be creative to study the scapes, since they provide the physical basis of the inscapes. For Hopkins the physical scape of poetry comprises the speech sounds. His concept may even be applied fruitfully to seeing poetry as 'the language of the body,' if we understand that for him the body in poetry speaks through its feelings and its sensibilities, and that for him these have sources deeper than those of physical sense. In their deeper source, found in a Christian-Platonic world, lie the origins of inscape. In the next chapter, which deals with poetry in its bodily character, I cite as an important parallel to Hopkins's concept of poeticalness Julia Kristeva's notion of 'poetic language.' In her materialist-Platonic plan the counterpart to the deeper sources of the poetic image resides in the psyche, in the Freudian id.

5 Poetry as the Language of the Body

It seems that Hopkins wrote substantially more poetry before he formulated sprung rhythm than he did afterward. Though he reports burning his poems in May 1868, when he decided on a religious life, enough remains of the early work to outweigh what was to come. Of the 179 poems gathered in the standard edition (P), 100 were composed before sprung rhythm. Yet most of the 100 are hardly known. Of them, only the brief *Heaven-Haven* (1864) and *Habit of Perfection* (1866) have drawn general critical interest. The contrast with the great celebrity of the later work is remarkable, and the reason seems clear-cut: sprung rhythm.

After entering the Jesuit novitiate in 1868 and before he adopted the new metrics in 1875 in *The Wreck of the Deutschland*, Hopkins professedly limited his verse composition to some 'presentation pieces' for church occasions (see LII 14). These pieces nevertheless offer sufficient evidence that his poetic sensibility underwent no dramatic transformation during that time. There are ten presentation poems in the edition, whose composition was spread out over the seven years of quasi-silence, virtually up to the date of *Deutschland*, and their style is very much of a piece with his previous verse. Nothing that he composed before *Deutschland*, aside from a few lines in *St. Dorothea*, anticipates sprung rhythm to any degree (see MacKenzie 1984), and nothing in those early works has the attraction as poetry of the later odes and sonnets. Something remarkable happened to his poetry in 1875, and it is surely not that the poet suddenly matured at age thirty-one, or that his reaction to the shipwreck deepened his sensibilities all at once. Rather, without doubt it was the formulation and adoption of sprung rhythm that caused Hopkins's verse composition to metamorphose from that of a competent Victorian writer to that of a master poet, whose work and whose theory look forward to a new age. In this chapter we will consider what it was about sprung rhythm that made the difference.

The first chapters of this study were devoted to analysis of sprung rhythm as a verse system whose chief aim is to reconcile the irregular rhythms of speech with the regular rhythms of verse. In chapter 2, especially, I noted that of the various aspects of his verse technique the main means he uses to bring about this meeting of verse and speech rhythms, by far the most important is his handling of stress. He asserts as much in various characterizations of his system, notably in stating flatly to Bridges, 'Stress is the life of sprung rhythm' (LI 52), and more expansively to his brother Everard, 'Sprung rhythm makes a verse stressy; it purges it to an emphasis ... much brighter than the regular but commonplace emphasis of common rhythm' (LIV 218). In his 'Note on the Rhythm' that accompanied the text of *Deutschland*, he advises the reader, 'strongly to mark the beats of the measure ... not disguising the rhythm and rhyme, as some readers do ... but laying on the beats too much stress rather than too little,' and he concludes the Note with the admonition: 'And so throughout let the stress be made to fetch out both the strength of the syllables and the meaning and feeling of the words' (P 118). The 'meaning and feeling' are dependent on the effectiveness of the physical utterance, speech stress. In the poet's sprung rhythm verse, much more than the earlier work, the lettering, especially the rhyme, reinforces the rhythmic stresses, bringing to the fore the material nature of the sound patterns. Such an emphasis accords with the value he accords to speech, spoken sound, particularly in 'Poetry and Verse' and his letter to Everard (LIV 218–19). Instead of the poetic text being merely a sequence of transparent symbols, the sound patterns give the text a physical opacity, and impart meaning to the sounds themselves.

This is not to say that Hopkins's reliance on material sound implies a materialist poetics; in his formulation, behind the physical scape lies the inscape. Nevertheless, the importance he attributes to material sound does lead to a surprising convergence between his idea of poetic language and that of the semiotician Julia Kristeva. Kristeva notably is influenced by Marx, Freud, and Lacan, thinkers far from Hopkins's sphere; but at the same time, in common with the poet, her ideas about language also have origins in Plato and the Greeks, and find support in the ideas of Charles Peirce and seminally those of Roman Jakobson. She emerged from the milieu of Eastern European theory in which Jakobson had a dominant place. As a result, there is a direct congruence between her impressively original theory of language meaning and Hopkins's equally original theory in that, while both recognize the logical meanings of language by which phonetic sounds are arbitrarily matched with meanings, both find that there is significantly more to the language systems and the poetry than these meanings.

Kristeva divides linguistic signification much as Hopkins implicitly divides poetic signification. She presents language meaning as having two strands, which she calls the *symbolic* and the *semiotic*. Her applications of this conventional terminology are hardly conventional. Kelly Oliver explains the two strands: 'The symbolic element is what philosophers might think of as meaning proper. That is, the symbolic is the element of signification that sets up the structures by which symbols operate.' This symbolic element has been the almost exclusive focus of many current phonologists. 'The semiotic element, on the other hand,' continues Oliver, 'is the organization of drives in language. It is associated with *rhythms and tones* that are meaningful parts of language and yet do not represent or signify something' (my emphasis). Or at least, 'the semiotic elements' are 'irreducible to the *symbolic element* of language' (Oliver in Kristeva 2002, xiv). While semiological theory does not recognize what she calls the 'semiotic' as part of language proper, Kristeva sees it as prior and basic, originating in bodily drives.

In asserting in 'Poetry and Verse,' that poetry is 'speech wholly or partially repeating some kind of figure over and above meaning, at least the grammatical, historical, and logical meaning' (J 289), Hopkins likewise postulates two areas of significance. Kristeva's 'symbolic' sense roughly corresponds to the overt kinds of meaning – logical and so on – that the poet says are ancillary to poeticality; his meaning 'over and above' is a counterpart to her semiotic. Both thinkers are more concerned with what is beyond, or prior to, the symbolic. Hopkins allows that 'some matter and meaning is essential' to poetry, though only in providing 'an element necessary to support and employ the shape.' For him it is the *shape* itself of the speech sounds that carries poeticality; as we have seen, this shape comprises the affective scapes that lead to inscape. Kristeva's 'semiotic' significances have a marked affinity to his 'shape' of the speech sounds that carries the affective inscape; and they also have priority in the linguistic process.

An important aspect of her writings stems from her work as a professional psychoanalyst, which she often applies in supporting her analysis of language as driven by 'material bodily processes,' that is, by affect. For her, 'All signification has material motivation.' Bodily drives 'move between *soma* and *psyche*, and the evidence of this movement is manifest in signification' (Oliver in Kristeva 2002, xvii). For Hopkins, comparably, despite his idealism, the inscape of speech, in which poetry resides, is an affective aspect of the bodily process that produces material speech: 'Poetry is in fact speech only employed to carry the inscape of speech for the inscape's sake' (J 289).

The content of both Hopkins's concept of the poetical and Kristeva's 'poetic language' is primarily affective, potentially applicable to all kinds of language use, in either prose or verse form. While for Hopkins the poetical is a feature of speech sound 'that is framed to be heard for its own sake and interest,' for Kristeva, whose major statement on language is entitled *Revolution in Poetic Language*, 'poetic language' concerns 'the infinite possibilities of language ... all other language acts [being] merely partial realizations of the possibilities inherent in "poetic language"' (Leon S. Roudiez in Kristeva 1984, 2). The infinitude of the possibilities for Kristeva, and the 'prepossession' or 'inscape' for Hopkins belong to a prior state in the act of language use when the affect, sensory urge, 'drive,' behind the developing verbal expression is present, but before the particular words have taken form.

The cosmologies underlying the respective theories of language are rooted in similar Platonic concepts. Krieteva sees language as beginning with a *chora*, 'a nonexpressive totality formed by the drives and their stases.' Remarking that she borrows the term *chora* from Plato's *Timaeus* 'to denote an essentially mobile and extremely provisional articulation,' she elaborates that '*chora* as rupture and articulations (rhythm), precedes evidence, verisimilitude, spatiality, and temporality' (1984, 25–6). In the *Timaeus, chora* is 'space,' the middle element in 'threefold nature, even before the heavens were created' (Plato, 186–7). The *chora* likewise is precedent in Kristeva's scheme: 'Neither model nor copy, the *chora* precedes and underlies figuration and thus specularization, and is analogous only to vocal or kinetic rhythm' (1984, 26). It is notable for present purposes that she speaks of the '(rhythmic and intonational) vocal modulations' as a particular feature of the '*semiotic* as a psychosomatic [i.e., connecting mind and body] modality of the semiotic process' (28–9). The semiotic is an aspect of speech sound that develops at an early stage in the process leading to an utterance. Not a static feature of linguistic superstructure, rather it is suited to participating in the affective poetic significance of speech sound.

For Hopkins, too, the affect enters early in the linguistic process. He tells Dixon that *Deutschland* had its inception in 'the new rhythm' that had been 'haunting' his 'ear' – not, then, in the first place his thought (LII 14). This suggests that analysis properly begins with discussion of the sound patterns and only afterwards should turn to the words that have subsequently materialized. The statements of diverse major poets that accord such precedence to sound features are almost a commonplace. The Muse typically communicates phonic inspiration, often in the form of a rhythm.

Paul Valéry's 'true story' of a rhythm taking hold of him provides a counterpart to Hopkins's description of the 'haunting' Muse; as pointed out by Michael Sprinker, Valéry recounts an experience while out for a walk. The physical aspect is salient in the narrative: 'As I went along the street where I live, I was suddenly *gripped* by a rhythm which took possession of me and soon gave me the impression of some force outside myself. It was as though someone else were making use of my *living-machine.* Then another rhythm overtook and combined with the first ... This composition became more and more complicated and soon in its complexity went far beyond anything I could reasonably produce with my ordinary, usable rhythmic faculties' (1958, 60–2; Sprinker 38 and n). The experience for him, Valéry indicates, was repeated on other occasions. His testimony, in turn, is comparable to T.S. Eliot's less vivid, more reasoned report that in his creative process rhythm often was precedent to the wording and inspired both the conception and the treatment: 'I know that a poem, or a passage of a poem, may tend to realise itself first as a particular rhythm before it reaches expression in words, and that this rhythm may bring to birth the idea and the image, and I do not believe that this is an experience peculiar to myself' (1942, 28). Rhythmic sound gives birth to a poem's word structure and meanings.

Independent reports of other poets repeatedly corroborate such testimony to the prime place of sound pattern. Seamus Heaney, in the course of writing on Wordsworth and Yeats, speaks of his own desire as a writer to explore 'the origins of a poet's characteristic music' and 'the relationship between the almost *physiological* operations of a poet composing and the music of the finished poem.' More precisely, he seeks out 'the way that certain postures and motions within the poet's incubating mind affect the posture of the voice and the motion of rhythms in the language of the poem itself' (Heaney 1980, 61; my emphasis). In another essay, Heaney finds W.H. Auden assigning coordinate import to verbal sound and verbal sense. Auden conceives poetry, he says, on the one hand as 'a matter of sound and the power of sound to bind our minds' and bodies' apprehensions within an acoustic complex,' and on the

other as 'a matter of making wise and true meanings.' In this conception, poems 'constitute temporary stays against the confusion threat-
ened by the mind's inclination to accept both accounts of the poetic
function in spite of their potential mutual exclusiveness' (1988, 109).
The 'acoustic complex' of poetic sound goes beyond rhythm to include
all aspects of language sound in its 'binding power.'

Rhythm, nonetheless, is the aspect of language sound that the poets
consistently emphasize. Thus, for the leading Soviet poet Vladimir
Mayakovsky 'rhythm is the basis' of any poem. He reports that his elegy
on the death of fellow poet Sergey Esenin began with a preverbal rhythm
that virtually materialized while he was walking. His description of the
process strongly recalls Valéry's having been physically possessed in his
walks by a rhythm, though direct influence is hardly likely:

> I walk along, waving my arms and mumbling almost wordlessly, now short-
> ening my steps so as not to interrupt my mumbling, now mumbling more
> rapidly in time with my steps.
>
> So the rhythm is trimmed and takes shape – and rhythm is the basis of any
> poetic work, resounding through the whole thing. Gradually individual
> words begin to ease themselves free of this dull roar ...
>
> More often than not the most important word emerges first: the word
> that most completely conveys the meaning of the poem, or the word that
> underlies the rhyme. (Mayakovsky 36)

He goes on to emphasize rhythm as 'the fundamental force, the fundamental energy of verse' (37).

Mayakovsky's subsequent elaboration of the genesis of his poems has a
further intriguing correspondence with a journal entry by a much earlier
poet, Percy Shelley. Both poets lay out patterns of specific rhythms and
then particular sounds in describing the emergence of their works. 'At
first,' says Mayakovsky, 'the poem to Esenin just rumbled away something like this:

> Ta-ra-rá/ra rá/ra ra ra rá/ra rá/
> ra-ra-ree/ra ra ra/ra ra/ra ra ra ra/
> ra-ra-ra/ra-ra ra ra ra ra raree
> ra-ra-ra/ra ra-ra/rara/ra/ra ra

'Then,' he continues, 'the words emerge.' In a further series of lines, in
which words intermingle with the meaningless syllables, he evokes the

materialization: 'You went off ra ra ra ra ra to a world above and so on' (38–9).

More than a century earlier, Shelley had recorded in his notebook several variously inchoate versions of *A Lament* ('O world, O life! O Time!'). Bennett Weaver characterizes one of these versions, which patently resembles Mayakovsky's grid of wordless syllables, as 'a rather elaborate study in symbols of rhythm' (Weaver 573–4):

Na na, na na na' na
Na na na na na – na na
Na na na na na na
Na na na na na a na

Na na na – na na – a na na
Na na na na – na na na na na
     Na na na na na
     Na na
Na na na na na
     Na na
Na na na na na – na!   (574)

On the notebook page opposite this pattern of sounds, and significantly in accord with the pattern, is an early half-verbal version of *A Lament*, similar to Mayakovsky's presentation of the developing poem, 'Ah time, oh night, oh day / Ni nal ni na, na ni,' and so on (Weaver 571). Weaver tentatively assumes that Shelley's symbols suggest a certain insistent rhythm and that the words on the opposite page are 'the result of an attempt to give this *beating pulse a body* in which to live' (574; my emphasis).

Assertions of the prior significance of poetic sound by two other poets, Robert Frost and the contemporary American Maya Angelou, focus on further aspects of speech sound that are independent of specific word meaning. I have previously cited Frost's statement that the 'abstract sound of sense' is basic to poetry, that is to say, a pre- or non-verbal meaning carried by a voice 'from behind a closed door,' which would be the speaker's emphases, intonations, and certain of the more distinctive letter sounds, aspects that mostly carry the affective content. Angelou, whose verse shows patent filiations with African-American folk poetry, points to another major aspect of poetic rhythm. Associating the rhythm with the natural cycles of the sun, moon, and tide, she says that in her verse composition she tries '*first* to find a rhythm' (Hagen 120).

World figures similarly look to innate natural origins to account for poetry's strength. Friedrich Nietzsche, inspired by Friedrich Schiller and joined by the Russian poets of the 1920s, finds it in the sound patterns of folk poetry. In *The Birth of Tragedy*, Nietzsche asserts that the repetitive metrics of folk verse have a Dionysian, innate power, and calls to witness Schiller's assertion that in his poetic creation musical sound precedes the emergence of the cognitive object: 'With me the perception has at first no clear and definite object; this is formed later. A certain musical mood comes first, and the poetical idea only follows later' (quoted in Nietzsche 1967, 49). Nietzsche, himself a poet, proceeds to claim: '*Melody is ... primary and universal*' (49, 53).

Like others who talk of verse 'music,' Nietzsche speaks of the melody of verse without differentiating verbal music from pitched music, though we might take the distinction as implicit in his discussion. Conflation of the two is valid in terms of the ancient definition of music as measured sound, if not in the more limited current understanding of music as pitched sound. Hopkins sees a common – overtly physical – origin for the two musics, agreeing with his contemporary Oxonian expert, Frederick Gore Ouseley, that the rhythms of the dance were the source of both pitched music and verse music (LI 119–20). Though on occasion Hopkins describes poetry and his own verse in terms of pitched music, he manifestly understands that, while the materials of the two musics are quite distinct, they particularly have in common rhythmic sound (J 273).

The poets' various statements about the phonetic and rhythmic beginnings of their works are quite explicit, and they provide compelling support for seeing foundational significance in the physical sound patterns of much of lyric verse. Accordingly, Hopkins's interests in the poetic tradition, expressed especially in his correspondence, to a remarkable extent concern metrics and related facets of the handling of sound. And, while his interest in sound patterns sometimes leads him in his verse to radically compressed expression and syntactical dislocation, he does not, as some assume, disregard coherent verbal meaning. Sprinker's association of Hopkins's poetry and poetics with Mallarmé's, with what Valéry called the great French poet's 'singular consuming mysticism,' is misleading (Sprinker 44; Valéry 1972, 426).

Hopkins was certainly a religious poet, but he was not a mystic, either a Catholic mystic like John of the Cross or a Romantic mystic (cf. J 83; Brown 17). His choice of the Jesuit order is indicative: not led to seek unmediated mystical understanding in monastic contemplation, he instead deliberately elected the Jesuits' socially oriented program of teaching and preaching (J 165; LIII 408). His poetic language, however compressed, is not meant to mystify, to be merely suggestive, or to produce phonetic effects for their own sake. Thus, he found inspiration and confirmation of his philosophical program in the writings of the arch-logical Duns Scotus, rather than in mystical authors. And the major models for his verse concepts and practice were the great classics, Pindar and Homer, Virgil and Ovid, Shakespeare and Milton, instead of the Romantics or his contemporaries, though, to be sure, he knew well and admired much of their work.

Furthermore, as Daniel Brown's study of the Hopkins archive shows, the poet was closely engaged with and knowledgeable about nineteenth-century science, especially physics (see esp. chaps 7–10). For him, as I have previously suggested, God's Book of the World was to be approached through scientific study. When he was observed staring fixedly at configurations of sand or clouds or focusing his perceptions narrowly on individual birds and trees, he was not in a mystical trance, nor in his preoccupation with separate phenomena was he primarily concerned with searching for the characteristically individual. Instead, as his notebooks and correspondence indicate, he was 'repeating the same energy on the same matter,' attempting to distinguish and contemplate the general forms within the particular phenomena – in Duns Scotus's terms, the designs of the common natures within the 'thisness' (haecceity) of the individuals. Early in life Hopkins seriously considered becoming a visual artist, and he devoted extended periods of time to sketching and drawing, especially nature studies. His strong interest in natural phenomena and in artistic representations of them no doubt was fundamental to his preoccupation with individual appearances, which his studies at Oxford stimulated and to which his later discovery of Duns Scotus's realism gave philosophical sanction that he found particularly satisfying.

The poet's physical and intellectual commitment to the phenomena of nature has a physical basis in common with his acute sensitivity to arrangements of material sound in verse. Both involve direct engagement with sensory experience. Just as his visual imagination inclined him early to painting and sketching, so his attraction to verbal sound and its patterns stimulated his great interest in prosody. Later on, he further displayed his aural sensibility by composing musical settings for his own verse and that of others. Though he felt his inexperience in music, that limitation did not keep him from more than elementary musical composition (see J. Stevens in J 457–63).

In speaking of the phonic origins of their work, the poets I have cited go beyond speaking of resemblance and explicitly align their poetry with music, at least in the important respect of rhythm. Contrary to the positivist tendencies in modern criticism that reject factors beyond empirical demonstration, on the basis of their personal experience these poets continued to believe in the capacity of poetry to unite with a source, speech sound, with rhythm primary, carrying the significance beyond the realm of verbal sense. Hopkins's explanation of how this happens is that the inscapes of the 'figures' of speech sound carry affective significance, meaningful feeling, which precedes the intellectual sense. The success of his sprung rhythm poetry offers pragmatic support for the theory, since its most distinctive characteristic is its highly original phonic patterning. Variations in stress pattern and metrical pace combine effectively with the well-ordered sequences of 'letter' sounds, which are marked by an exceptional concentration of alliteration, vowel gradation, and complex end-rhyme.

Critical analysis of his poetry, nevertheless, has concentrated heavily on its discursive sense, and even the best analysts of his work have not attended to the effects of the prosodic patterns. Most theorists adhere to a mimetic view of the value of language sound, which leads to their assuming that the worth of the sound in literature depends largely on its support of the lexical meaning, thus to the doctrine expressed in Pope's aphorism, 'the sound must be an echo of the sense.' But sound-sense relations in language, at least those that are demonstrable, are not especially impressive in total, though they are often individually compelling. Roman Jakobson's essay 'The Spell of Speech Sounds' is valuable as a comprehensive review of the significant relations of word sound to word meaning, but as a demonstration that language sound has broad effect on lexical or logical meaning, or suggests anything like an onomatopoetic theory of language, it is, in total, disappointing.

Hopkins evidently early came to the conclusion that, while speech sound has important significance for language, it does not primarily lie in onomatopoeia and comparable sound-sense relations. Rather it arises independently from the patterns of the sound figures. But language theory dominant today presents a serious stumbling block to the poet's formulations, as well as to the implicit faith that poets and students of literature for millenia have accorded to metrics and sound repetitions. One can hardly accept that language sound has no positive systematic significance, as the prevailing theory maintains, and still believe that metrics and other aspects of sound patterning, especially in poetry, have integral importance.

In the prevalent view, nonetheless, sound differentials that are arbitrarily fixed almost solely determine verbal sense, lexical and grammatical meanings. Of themselves the material sounds of language have no value for fixing linguistic meaning, the expressive features of oral presentation being controlled by the speaker and lacking the systematic significance appropriate to language proper. Gérard Genette, quoting Saussure, paraphrases the latter's thesis and draws out its consequences: 'If we are not "dealing with a substance when we deal with linguistic phenomena" but only with "conventional values" that are "distinct from the tangible element which serves as their vehicle" without being able to determine them "any more than metal or paper does the value of money"; if the linguistic signifier is "*not physical* in any way" but "constituted solely by differences which distinguish one ... sound pattern from another," it necessarily follows that this signifier in its essence, does not belong to the phonic order any more than to other material orders. Therefore, it is "*impossible that sound, as a material element, should in itself be part of language.* Sound is simply something ancillary, a material that language [*langue*] uses"' (330; my emphases).

Literary theorists have creatively found a way to accept both the validity of such analysis *as well as* the positive value in sound patterns. They posit that poetry's devices help to form a 'secondary modelling system,' which imparts to the forms of literature the special meaning felt by most readers and most theorists. Twentieth-century analysts such as Jurij Lotman and William K. Wimsatt, whose ideas about language sound I discussed in chapter 3, are among those who posit a special literary 'modelling system.' But these theorists pass over the difficulty of defining how much metre, imagery, fictional framing, and so on it takes to effect the transformation of ordinary language into poetry, what might form the dividing line. They also pass over strong evidence that the poetic, at least as Hopkins, along with Kristeva and Jakobson, define it, is integral to language. For them the poetic is a potential aspect of all language use. In introducing Kristeva's *Revolution in Poetic Language*, Leon S. Roudiez notes that Kristeva does not see 'poetic language' as 'a sub-code of the linguistic code [i.e., a secondary system]. Rather it stands for the infinite possibilities of language, and all other language acts are merely partial realizations of the possibilities inherent in poetic language' (1984, 2).

Hopkins specifically sees the inscape of *speech sound* as potentially conveying major poetic significance. He holds that the meanings of a poem are not – or should not be – matters for the speaker's ultimate judgment, but rather that they are integral aspects of language bearing an import based on the poet's spoken text. Hopkins in his own work uses diacritical marks to control such meaning when he senses that they are needed. While the phonemic contrasts indeed tell us that '*t*ake' and '*m*ake' have different symbolic meanings, and that together with myriad other contrasts they determine the logical sense of each lexical item in fine detail, Hopkins's conception of language points especially to a further fundamental property of linguistic significance that in his terms points to its 'inscape' or 'prepossession of feeling.' It involves the human values that both intrinsic phonetic qualities and accretive usage attach to the sounds of a meaningful utterance.

Roman Jakobson as linguist and critic was much concerned with language sound. One result was that among prominent theorists only he recognized Hopkins as a major thinker about poetics, finding in his writings a 'prodigious insight into the structure of poetry' (1987, 82). Indeed, Hopkins early applied his fine theoretical mind to general linguistic issues, especially as regards poetic meaning. His thinking about language was fortified by extensive study of the classical languages and literatures and by his own sharp linguistic observation, especially of phonetic aspects. His student diaries (1863–4) show a lively interest in sound symbolism that led him to muse that 'the onomatopoetic theory [of language origin] has not had a fair chance' (J 5). But while his word lists indicate a growing interest in language sound and have a suggestive connection with the numerous sequences of alliterating words found in his later poetry, sound symbolism did not remain an obvious feature of his interests. When in his surviving writings the young poet again focused his attention specifically on language, he did so in two short essays, one on Wordsworth's ideas about poetic diction (1865; J 85–6) and the other the essay on word meanings 'All words ...' (1868; J 125–30), which is particularly significant for his developing theory. In these essays and afterwards the focus of his linguistic reflections turned increasingly from concern with word sense to phonetic matters. His main and abiding linguistic preoccupation became a notably poetic one: speech-sound systems, especially rhythm.

Hopkins did not finally settle on his own early privileging of parallelism as the identifying element of poetry. Rather, he came to theorize, most notably in 'Poetry and Verse' (J 289–90), that parallelism is the mark of *verse*, not poetry, with verse being an important facilitator of poetical insight but not of the poetic essence. Jakobson evidently did not read 'Poetry and Verse,' and he took an essentially mimetic view of verse sound. His late summary essay, 'The Spell of Speech Sounds,' treating mimetic aspects, hardly succeeds in showing, as he aspires to show, that they are pervasive in language generally or poetry specifically. Likewise, as regards poetry, while William Wimsatt's demonstration in 'One Relation of Rhyme of Reason' (1954, 152–66), in which he cites Pope's 'wedding of the logical with the alogical' in the rhyme words (e.g., a china jar's 'flaw' with 'Diana's law' of chastity), offers several compelling examples of one kind of direct sound/sense connection, yet the total of similar rhyme contrasts in first-rate rhymed poetry is quite limited. In both Jakobson's and Wimsatt's essays an implicit assumption that direct sound/meaning relationships are ubiquitous is not borne out.

Hopkins, to the contrary, while allowing that 'Some matter and meaning is essential [to poetic language],' states explicitly that it is 'only as an element necessary to support and employ the shape which is *contemplated for its own sake*' (J 289; my emphasis). This shape, he maintains, is properly perceived in expressive oral presentation of the poetry that captures the speech rhythms inherent in the poet's text (not in the readers' various interpretations). Kristeva's reports of Jakobson's efforts to capture the sounds of the Soviet writers' readings, '*imitating* their voices, with the lively rhythmic accents' (cited above in chapter 1; my emphasis) shows his inherent agreement that the poet's own conception of the sound scape of his work, as well as his writen text, is authoritative. There are, of course, variable factors of the external sound scape that depend on the presenter, such as quality of voice, which bear on the effect of oral presentation of poetry; but it is not these that lead to the inscape. Rather, it is controllable meaningful factors, such as the patterns of rhythm, tone, and emphasis, which our writing system only partially is designed to represent.

Hopkins's formulation of his ideas about the precedence of poetic sound is opposed not only to current strictures of linguistic theory that limit the role of language sound, but also to the broad twentieth-century acceptance by literary theorists of the concept of the poem as an integral icon in which the sound value is subsumed in the representation. This subsumption finds its strongest support in Aristotle's theory of mimesis. Hopkins well knew the theory, as he shows in his lecture notes for 'Rhythm and the Other Structural Parts of Rhetoric – Verse.' He explains the theory without partisan comment, stating that Aristotle sees all *poiesis*, creative art, as mimesis, 'imitation, reproduction, representation, and he says this of verse, music, and dancing. The imitation or representation is of character, feeling and action.' He notes that Aristotle discusses the uses of various metres: iambs for action, trochees for narrative, and so on. This leads to a discourse on the 'particular character' of various 'feet and rhythms.' The only point in the *Poetics* relevant to Hopkins's own theory is the connection of iambic rhythm with 'the language of common talk' (J 273–4).

Hopkins's comment about mimesis is neutral, specifically neither agreeing nor disagreeing, but clearly 'imitation of an action' conceived in the usual way is not what the poet sees as central to lyric poetry. Applied to all aspects of literature, mimesis suggests that in all poetry the sounds should be aimed towards the imitation of an action thereby implying a radical subordination of sound's significance to word meaning; in that respect it is an onomatopoetic theory of language sound. Holding such a view, Aristotle in the *Poetics* logically ranks plot, character, thought, and diction as being of prior importance to metre – sound pattern. Application of mimetic theory to lyric poetry is particularly problematical for Hopkins's idea.

Hopkins expresses his ideas about the centrality of speech sound in poetry in notably original terms, but at the same time his concepts evidence the influence of a wide range of classical sources. His diaries show he had read the *Poetics* by his first year at Balliol, though it did not become important for his poetic theory. In his lecture notes for 'Verse,' he cites from the *Poetics* only the secondary discussion of metre. Aristotle's *Rhetoric* is more relevant to the poet's ideas about speech sound, and more basic still are the discourses of other ancient rhetoricians.

Hopkins's foregrounding of speech sound and his enthusiasm for the power of prose effects have natural precedents in classical rhetoric and its tradition of *ars metrica*. He well knew that the esteem of Greek and Roman thinkers for spoken rather than written discourse went beyond Plato's denigration of writing in the *Phaedrus* to imputation of special power to rhetorical presentation. Classical rhetoricians other than Plato and Aristotle laid particular stress on the affective content of spoken word-sounds. Stephen Katz notes the tendency, manifested in treatises from the sophists and Isocrates through Cicero, by which rhetoricians attributed a 'phonocentric' rather than 'logocentric' affective power to speech utterance. Katz asserts that a 'poetic tradition of rhetoric that developed from early oral verse and song through oratorical eloquence to sensuous written prose, in which the music of rhetoric was epistemic ... can be traced from the pivotal first sophists up through Cicero, whose later rhetorical treatises may represent the mature culmination of the sophistic "literary tradition"'(85). Developing from verse practice in early classical Greece, rhetoric theory retained the concern of the poets for the affective power of sound. Isocrates, in particular, 'facilitated and continued the transition from poetry to prose begun by the early sophists, the development of a literary rhetoric that retained the oral, "musical" modes of thought' (99).

It is nevertheless another tradition of ancient thought, *ars musica*, which most directly implicates sound in poetic values and is of primary importance for Hopkins's theory. Classical arts of music see poetry as music and assume that verbal representation is not where the main value lies. *Ars musica*, then, conceives poetry as Hopkins does, as arranged sound, in which lexical meaning is important only 'as an element necessary to support and employ the shape [of the sound]' (J 289). For *ars musica*, poetry is a major class of music located on a sonic continuum with pitched music. Sound pattern being primary in verse as in pitched music, sound carries important independent significance. St Augustine's treatise on music, *De Musica* (fourth century), which Hopkins cites and quotes as an authority, was a prime transmitter of the concept of poetry as music to the Middle Ages and beyond. Into the Renaissance, of course, poetry was conceived, like music, as necessarily involving patterns of performed physical sound.

Augustine's dictum that music is 'ars bene modulandi' (the art of measuring sound well) presents it as embracing equally verse and pitched music. Accordingly, medieval treatises on verse often present poetry as music of two kinds, one based on classical metrics, the other on accentual prosody. Cassiodorus's influential *Institutiones* (sixth century) notably distinguishes *musica metrica* that follows the time measure of classical verse, and *musica rhythmica* that divides verse into accentual feet with the lines usually rhymed (see Crocker). John of Garland's thirteenth-century *The Parisiana Poetria* distinguishes three kinds of 'instrumental music,' two of them being rhymed stress verse and quantitative verse, with the human voice being the instrument that performs poetry (158–61). Similarly, Dante associates lyric poetry closely with music. He defines the canzone as 'harmonized words for a musical setting,' with accompanying musical notation *not* required to fulfil the form (49). Eustache Deschamps in his *Art de dictier* (1392) extends the connection between poetry and music, creatively defining pitched music as 'artificial music' and verse as 'natural music' (7:270–1). The close association of poetry with music carried through the Renaissance. In Milton's *Paradise Lost*, as Hardison asserts, the fact that the Muse *sings* of 'things invisible to mortal sight,' offers 'a powerful reassertion of the ancient theory that poetry is constitutive and that its power comes to it through music' (22). Thus, the tradition of music theory implicitly accords to the sound patterns of verse basic significance apart from its verbal representation.

Although his attribution of independent significance, 'epistemic' effect, to speech sound no doubt was influenced by his study of classical rhetoric, there is the definitive difference that rhetoricians applied the affective 'musical' power to rhetorical ends (which is to say, for persuasion), while for Hopkins the power was for poetical purposes, a 'musical' power attached to the spoken sounds, producing affective meaning precedent to – over and above – verbal sense. His ideas looked back past the time when prose rhetoric developed from verse to the very origins of poetry and music in the rhythms of the dance. Though St Augustine's *De Musica* is a work of lesser scope and originality than the *Poetics*, its subject and treatment are closer to Hopkins's interests. He adduces as authoritative Augustine's metrical discussions (J 273, 444–5), and he also cites his treatment of metrical proportion (LII 71–2). Rhythm and metre, poetic sound rather than plots, are the poet's abiding interest and also his great talent.

In the Renaissance, Aristotle's theory of mimesis became prominent in literary theory, and it came to dominate neoclassical thought: the essence of art is imitation; the painter and poet are to imitate and adorn nature. Pope, while warning against a too rigid application of 'Aristotle's rules' (*Essay on Criticism*, lines 263–84), assumes that the function of verse art is enhancement of Nature, 'True wit is Nature to advantage dressed' (line 297). Consequently, in verse, 'The sound must seem an echo to the sense' (line 365). He famously illustrates the maxim with his own poetic descriptions of the strength of Ajax and the swiftness of Camilla, of gentleness and roughness (lines 364–83). Though he habitually refers to poetry by the interestingly musical terms, 'numbers,' in *Essay on Criticism* he nevertheless expresses contempt for 'tuneful fools' who would judge the poem by its music:

> But most by numbers judge a poet's song;
> And smooth or rough with them is right or wrong:
> In the bright muse though thousand charms conspire,
> Her voice is all these tuneful fools admire,
> Who haunt Parnassus but to please their ear,
> Not mend their minds; as some to church repair,
> Not for the doctrine, but the music there.   (337–43)

For Pope, it seems, religion and poetry are primarily rational affairs, not fraught with non-verbal significances, so that the affective experience of music has marginal relevance to church-going.

In *Essay on Criticism*, as noted above, Pope likens the 'nameless graces' of poetry that are beyond the reach of art to those of music (lines 297–8). In this respect, he says, poetry 'resembles' music (lines 143–5). But his alignment of the two arts later in the *Essay* is based on mimesis, musical representation of emotions, not the innate values of music. He calls to witness Dryden's *Alexander's Feast*, which depicts the harp of Timotheus as by turns inciting Alexander to rage, lulling him, and leading him finally to sadness through musical evocations of the successive moods. Through the metrical imitation of emotion, Pope says, Dryden's verse exerts the same emotive power that he attributes to Timotheus's music: 'what Timotheus was is Dryden now' (line 383). This attitude passes to twentieth-century doctrines of New Criticism and structuralism. Nevertheless, in the nineteenth century the neoclassical canons were by no means accepted universally. The prestige and the continued emphasis of the educational system on Greek and Latin literature, especially metrical poetry, ensured that a preoccupation with prosody and its consequent foregrounding of sound continued through the century.

Hopkins' discussions of poetry with his three main poet-correspondents, Bridges, Dixon, and Patmore, deal largely with matters of metre and rhythm. They implicitly accept that sound patterns are basic. Similarly the testimony of the poets I cited above, who report the priority of wordless rhythm in their creative experience, stands in contrast to the typical mimetic conception of poetry by which the verse treatment is tailored to a precedent rhetorical plan. Any value that sound has in poetry, it is assumed, must arise from its contribution to the representation. Mimesis, as currently understood, is not hospitable to a concept such as that of Hopkins that poetry is a rhythmic arrangement of speech sound constitutive of an otherwise inexpressible reality.

The effect that the canons of current linguistics has had on attribution of independent poetic value to sound – a special significance beyond its lexical sense – is witnessed by a comment of the poet-critic, Octavio Paz, which I quoted more fully in chapter 1. Paz is led to doubt his innate conviction that sound and sense are allied metaphysically: 'It is only with great antipathy that I accept (provisionally) the fact that the relation between sound and meaning ... is the result of an arbitrary convention.

My misgivings are natural: poetry is born of the age-old magic belief in the identity of the word and what it names' (quoted in Heaney 1999, 14).

It is not possible to know how Hopkins, had he lived, would have responded to a theory that arbitrary sound differentials comprise language, but his writings up to the time of his death amount to a cogent argument that there is more to it than that. For him the physical sounds of speech, in addition to bearing the ('grammatical, historical, and logical') meanings identified negatively by sound differentials, also carry a 'prepossession of feeling' that is stable – not dependent on the speaker's independent conception – and of vital significance for poetic language. Spoken language has not only a 'scape,' an outer phonetic shell, but also an 'inscape' that is the essential property of poetry. Poetry is a material artefact, 'speech framed for contemplation of the mind ... to be heard for its own sake and interest even over and above its interest of meaning' (J 289).

It is a theory worthy both of the realist and idealist that Hopkins early became and always remained and of the passionate lover of the physical world describing the music of the ascending lark:

His rash-fresh re-winded new-skeinèd score
In crisps of curl off wild winch whirl, and pour
And pelt music, till none's left to spill nor spend.   (*The Sea and the Skylark*, 6–8)

Though he found it 'dreadful to explain these things in cold blood' (P 374), Hopkins carefully translated these lines for Bridges, which in their untranslated state nevertheless comprise a meaningful physical artefact presenting a poet-musician bird and its 'new-skeinèd' score.

Conclusion:
'The Music of His Mind' –
Hopkins's Poetry and His Poetics

Hopkins's poetic texts, even more than his diaries and correspondence, provide compelling evidence that the poet's sensory experiences and his responses to them were exceptionally intense. His most celebrated sprung rhythm lyrics evidently were written in two surges of emotional energy. The first issued in a series of sonnets composed shortly after his ordination in 1877, which describe in highly charged figurative terms a 'kingdom of daylight' that in one way or another reflects a loving and all-encompassing deity, poems such as *God's Grandeur, Pied Beauty*, and *The Windhover*. The second produced the series of Dark Sonnets, composed around 1884–6, when he had been assigned to Dublin, which relate experiences in a night-time world in which the deity is remote or forbidding.

With both sets, the figurative language is exceptionally vivid, often synaesthetic: euphoric images, 'shining from shook foil,' 'ooze of oil / crushed,' 'daylight's dauphin, dapple-dawn-drawn Falcon,' 'blue-bleak embers ... gash gold-vermillion,' 'swift, slow; sweet, sour; adazzle, dim'; and, in stark contrast, images of deep dejection, 'the fell of dark, not day,' 'I am gall, I am heartburn,' 'More pangs will, schooled at forepangs, wilder wring,' 'on an age-old anvil wince and sing,' 'Not, I'll not, carrion comfort, Despair, not feast on thee.'

His long and wide experiences in the arts, his walks and sketching in the countryside, his early reading of Ruskin and study of architecture cultivated the poet's naturally acute aesthetic sensitivities. That instress and inscape are matters of feeling – 'the great moving power and spring of verse' (LI 66) – certainly accords with his temperament. His synaesthetic sensibility shows up particularly in his defence of William Barnes's poetry on the basis of their 'Westcountry instress.' The verse evoked for Hopkins variously landscapes, folk songs, artful verse of the region, and '*above all* ... the *smell* of oxeyes and applelofts' (LI 88; my emphasis).

Smells for him are not perceptions secondary to those of sight and hearing. His broad trans-sensory characterization suggests that inscape involves a common denominator of sense perceptions, a main aspect of the 'common natures' that form the physical world.

When Hopkins was entering his final year at Oxford, Benjamin Jowett, master of Balliol, assigned Walter Pater, then a fellow of Brasenose, to give the poet 'intensive coaching' to help him to prepare for his finals (White 131). Pater was Hopkins's senior by only five years, and the relationship between the two obviously developed beyond tutoring to more personal philosophical discussion; in one meeting, the poet reports, Pater talked 'two hours against Xtianity' (132). Obviously, the tutor did not carry his anti-Christian arguments, but neither, apparently, was Hopkins markedly offended. Against even Pater's impressive learning and eloquence, the poet had calm confidence in his own convictions, and a friendly relationship between the two continued after Hopkins completed his university studies. In contrast to their opposed religious beliefs, Pater's aesthetic awareness seems quite in accord with Hopkins's own. His familiar formulation, 'All art constantly aspires to the condition of music,' could be applied to proposing that for Hopkins the inscape of art, its common nature, is an 'arch-music.' That all forms of art strive towards the status of wordless music is notably compatible with the poet's synaesthetic sensitivity and his emphasis on the inscape of the physical sound of speech as the basis of poetry.

If one assumes that Hopkins's inscape is a common element of the various arts and can be identified as a 'music,' moreover, then not only is poetry like pitched music in being a matter of organized sound, coming under the classical view of poetry as a variety of music, but also the visual and plastic arts join it in emphasizing qualities that are characteristic of music. The text and textual circumstances of a poem that Hopkins composed, which extols in musical terms an imposing old stone building, probably a Gothic structure, dramatically supports thinking the verse a conscious application of Pater's dictum. It is especially indicative that the preferred version of the poem's second stanza is written in a space above an 1879 letter that Pater sent to Hopkins accepting an invitation to dinner (MS II, pl. 354). I quote the first three of thirteen quatrains:

Who shaped these walls has shewn
The music of his mind,
Made known, though thick through stone,
What beauty beat behind.

How all's to one thing wrought!
The members, how they sit!
O what a tune the thought
Must be that fancied it.

Though down his being's bent
Like air he changed in choice,
That was an instrument
Which overvaulted voice.   (1–12; P 159–60)

In the variant versions of lines 7–8 the architect's concept is a 'tune' that
'trod' to 'a measure,' or a 'thought' that has, alternatively, musical
'measures,' or 'motions.' The poem presents music as in the first place
an inclusive mental phenomenon, a matter of proportion, but directed
to 'one thing,' an archetypal 'tune' in the architect's mind that the
structure itself 'made known.' This kind of imagery clearly had a special
expressiveness for Hopkins.

The concluding stanza of 'Who shaped these walls' underlines what
is implicit in the preceding stanzas, that it is not in the old building's
external appearance, its 'rind,' that its greatest beauties, its 'brightest
blooms,' reside, but in the concealed virtue of its 'sweetest nectar':

Who built these walls made known
The music of his mind,
Yet here he has but shewn
His ruder-rounded rind.
His brightest blooms lie there unblown
His sweetest nectar hides behind.   (37–42)

The nectar, we must think, is the inscape that can be drawn out by the
affective faculties.

In 'Poetry and Verse' Hopkins states that figures of speech sound
arranged so as to 'to carry the inscape of speech for the inscape's shape'
convey the poetical nucleus. He implicates all features of speech sound,
but rhythm has precedence. Its logaoedic, prose-poetic nature makes it
able to accommodate not only Whitman's free verse, but also the least
formal of recent poetry. In certain speech-sound contexts a poem can
carry the inscape of speech without the repetitions of verse; in these
cases '*once* of the inscape will be enough for art and beauty and poetry.'
Prose, too, can qualify; though 'debarred' from verse's 'symmetrical

beauties,' it 'has at least possible to it, effects more beautiful than any verse can attain' (LIV 220). But whether verse or prose, a text that is poetical must be spoken. Poeticalness resides in speech sound.

Was Hopkins himself in the 1880s moving away from traditional forms towards a 'logaoedic' verse akin to that of Walt Whitman? It seems not. His last several poems, including the very last, *To R.B.*, are sonnets of quite regular form. Furthermore, Hopkins quite emphatically denied that the metrics of *The Leaden Echo and the Golden Echo* (1882), with its irregular line lengths, were, as Bridges suggested, 'like Whitman,' and instead declares the verse to be like that of Pindar (LI 154–58; P 429). *Echoes* was designed as a part of a tragedy, *St. Winefred's Well*, which Hopkins worked on sporadically from 1879 until 1886, three years before his death. The several other fragments that survive (presented in P as poem 153) are in 124 unrhymed long lines; at first glance their metrics look irregular, but the poet's division of each long verse with a short horizontal bar evidences a careful metrical plan, a sprung rhythm design equivalent to Alexandrines 'in accordance with Patmore's dipodic theory' (P 440).

Even regarding the irregular line lengths of *Echoes*, Hopkins insisted that he was attentive to the regularity of the foot timing; he declared that, if readers took account of both length and strength, they would find rhythmic regularity. This attention to timing and his use of the annotations and techniques of pitched music, which in his later compositions markedly increased in frequency, offer further indication that he did find independent values in the repetitions of verse form. 'Poetry and Verse' itself suggests the aesthetic contributions of verse form: rhythm imparts 'tone' and '*candorem*' (clarity), while lettering concurrently conveys 'brilliancy' (J 290). Though finished speakers often cultivate rhetorical effects through rhyming and alliteration, Hopkins's intensiye lettering in his verse only secondarily is a speechlike or logaoedic aspect of his poetry; its primary contribution is to the uniformity of verse, making more prominent the verse repetition and closely implicating the segmental or letter sounds in the metrical scheme.

The forms of *Echoes* and *St. Winefred's Well*, while they do not indicate a radical new direction for Hopkins's poetic structures, reflect his almost restless experimenting with verse form that is especially characteristic of the years between *Echoes* in 1882 and *That Nature Is a Heraclitean Fire* in 1888. During these years he did produce some fine works that did not involve substantial formal variation from previous sprung rhythm works. The Dark Sonnets, which came 'like inspirations unbidden,' are notable among them. They make highly effective use of the proven resources of the form without further experimentation.

Yet in the same years he composed two of his most ambitious and outstanding experimental works: *Spelt from Sybil's Leaves*, a chant made up of weighty eight-foot lines, and the thrice 'caudated' *Heraclitean Fire*. These are at the same time superb expansions of the sonnet form and explorations of the lyric potential of sprung rhythm. Hopkins's variety of poetic activity also produced lyrics in Latin and Greek and several meditative sonnets in standard rhythm. In 1887 he wrote the semi-successful trio of unusual metrical experiments that I have previously discussed: the pair of sonnets, *Harry Ploughman*, in sprung rhythm with six interspersed burden-lines, and *Tom's Garland*, in standard rhythm but counterpointed and with two codas; and *Ashboughs*, a curtal sonnet in alexandrines. In these poems he is shown to be experimenting not only by the expansions and contractions of the sonnet form, but especially by his unusually heavy use of special metrical effects – marked by rounded ties under the lines indicating outrides, rounded ties over three or more syllables designating half-feet, and marks directing that monosyllables should be made disyllables – indications of the poet's aspirations to a further prosodic music, of his desire to explore other untapped veins of verse that would capitalize on the possibilities that he had opened with sprung rhythm. He himself describes the portraits of Harry and Tom as 'works of infinite, of over great contrivance' (LII 153), suggesting intensive testing of technical resources. Fascinating as poetic experiments, they are not major exemplars in Hopkins's oeuvre.

Although *Sybil's Leaves* and *Heraclitean Fire* are splendid works, metrically they led to dead ends. After he composed the latter work in July 1888, the few poems that Hopkins wrote in his remaining ten months of life show no further probing after new poetic form. It may be that the 'one rapture of an inspiration' that he longs for in his valedictory *To R.B.* refers not to fresh poetic matter, but to new rhythmic progress for his verse towards an archetypal 'condition of music,' a forward movement beyond the territories that sprung rhythm had opened to him.

Hopkins has left us a relatively small, very valuable body of significant poetry that itself is *sui generis*. At the same time, in addition to yielding the pleasure and profit of great poetry, the poetry stands as illustration and vindication of his ambitious poetics, which perhaps best show his modernity. In finding overriding poetic value in the sounds of speech, the poet foregrounds the sensory and affective –'alogical' – features of language: in the feeling, the sense of the affective consciousness that is inherent in the vocal articulation of the poem; in the stress and intonation; in 'O' and 'Ah,' as much icon as conventional symbol; and in the feeling attached to the segmental phones and their combinations into syllables and further evoked by the strings of syllables that constitute words and sentences. Other theoreticians that I have cited have argued similarly that language has an important non-logical aspect. Julia Kristeva speaks of 'a semiotic rhythm that no system of linguistic communication has yet been able to assimilate.' A proper system, she says, 'would establish *poetic language* as the object of linguistics' attention in its pursuit of truth in language' (1980, 24–5). Her characterization of 'poetic language' importantly recalls Jakobson's formulation of the 'emotive' or 'poetic' function of language that he associates particularly with lyric poetry and its orientation towards the first person, Hopkins's poetic territory (Jakobson 1987, 69–71).

In accord with Hopkins's conception of the poetical, the significances that attach to the poetic function of language that Jakobson and Kristeva identify are based in speech sound, not in symbolic verbal meanings. I have already cited a similar privileging of sound pattern in Friedrich Nietzsche's *Birth of Tragedy out of the Spirit of Music,* and in the treatise and poems that he collected under the title of the medieval Provençal poetics, *The Gay Science* (*Die fröliche Wissenschaft*). In *Birth of Tragedy,* Nietzsche proposes that, while the linguistic statement of Greek tragedy is inherently 'Apollonian,' that is, orderly and logical, the musical element in which tragedy and lyric are born is Dionysian, suitable to probing the chaotic nature that underlies the apparent order of the world. He adds to Friedrich Schiller's statement that he began a poem with a '*musical* mood' that, unlike verbal statements, music involves no presentation of phenomena but, citing Schopenhauer, it presents 'an immediate copy of the will itself' (1974, 49; my emphasis). The tragic actions, though presented in the logical structures of language, penetrate to the deeper forces that constantly threaten to engulf each of us.

Nietzsche cites the development of tragedy from danced and sung lyric forms as evidence that lyric poetry in general develops from music's striving 'to express its nature in Apollonian images' – verbal images – despite its basically Dionysian, non-verbal character (1967, 103). His own lyric poem entitled *Poet's Conceit* (*Dichter-Eitelkeit*), found in *The Gay Science* collection, posits that non-logical prosody integrates poetic words into a musical matrix and dominates the verbal logic:

Just give me glue; then for the glue	Gebt mir nur Leim; denn zur Leime
I myself soon will find wood.	Find'ich selber mir schon Holz!
To put meaning into four	Sinn in vier unsinn'ge Reime
meaningless rhymes	Legen – ist kein kleiner Stolz!
Is no small glory!	

(1974, 'Prelude,' no. 56)

The 'glue' is the music, pitched or prosodic (here, the 'Reime'), which, despite its lacking lexical or grammatical meaning (and being therefore 'unsinn'ge'), holds the wood ('Holz') of the verbal statement together. In his poem, as in folk song, he is asserting, it is especially the stanza form that glues it together, imparting wordless significance to the succession of stanzas, whose sequence often has little logic. In the song the melody is '*primary and universal,* and so may admit of several objectifications in several texts ... Melody generates the poem out of itself, ever again: This is what the *strophic form of the folk song signifies*' (1967, 53).

Statements of the various prominent poets that I have cited testify to their sense that rhythm is precedent in poetic creation; their accord with Nietzsche's concept of the development of the choruses of tragedy and lyric poetry from music is significant. The testimony of all of them, as well as Kristeva's and Jakobson's assertion of the poetic function of language, is in harmony with Hopkins's notion of a poetic meaning that is over and above the grammatical and logical sense of the words. Poetry as well as pitched music is born, in the first place, in feeling, the affective consciousness, and the feeling latent in the inscape of the sound patterns is what poetry as poetry primarily conveys.

Hopkins's ideas are similar to Nietzsche's in their attributing independent affective meaning to poetic sound patterns. The poet identifies as inscape what the affective consciousness finds through its single-minded contemplation of the sound pattern: 'Poetry is in fact speech only employed to carry the inscape of speech for the inscape's sake' (J 289). We may legitimately locate a certain compatibility with inscape in Nietzsche's conception of the Dionysian, but of course Hopkins found the best explanation of his concept in the realism of John Duns Scotus. At the same time, it is not Scotus's idea of haecceity (thisness) that is most basic to inscape, as critics have sometimes assumed, but rather his concept of formalities, the shared forms that make up the individual. Hopkins prized the singularity of the 'counter, original, spare, strange,' not for the strangeness itself, but instead for the eminently distinctive embodiments of the common natures. For Hopkins, sprung rhythm,

which achieves a reconciliation of the apparently incompatible idiosyncratic rhythms of speech with the regularity of verse, follows along the
path of Scotus's reasoning, which reconciles the individuality of haecceity
with the common natures of the formalities. As Louis Mackey says, 'The
"inscape" that Hopkins speaks of is (loosely) the network of forms that
you see when you look into a thing through its *haecceity*' (Mackey 179).

The forms of the 'inscape' are only indirectly related to the forms of a
'scape' apprehended by physical perceptions; for inscape requires the
mind's inner eye. Scotus's formalities and haecceity are metaphysical
concepts, and apprehension of them is available only to contemplation
'in which the mind is absorbed [in] a single thought' (J 126). The
repetitions of verse abet such contemplation. Hopkins uses sprung rhythm
to devise the necessary repetitions while retaining the naturalness of
speech in which inscape is embedded; nevertheless, the poet conceives
his sprung rhythm versification as only one possible application of his
poetics of speech sound. His definition of poetry allows for a wide range
of verbal structures that can 'carry the inscape of speech for the inscape's
sake.' It defines a poetics that is applicable to all lyric poetry, not to his
alone.

It may be that between the composition of 'Poetry and Verse' in 1873
or 1874 and that of his more metrically complex and musical poems such
as *Spelt from Sybil's Leaves* and *Harry Ploughman* in the mid- and late 1880s,
Hopkins had moderated his view of poeticalness as constituted solely by
speech sound and come to see verse regularity as making an important
basic contribution to the essence of poetry. However this may be, there is
a surprising consistency in his envisaging poetry as potentially constituted in a broad spectrum of speech discourse. Only four years before he
died, in his letter to Everard he is even more emphatic than in his
prefaces on rhythm and in 'Poetry and Verse' about the alliance of
poetry and speech: 'Sprung rhythm gives back to poetry its true soul and
self. As poetry is emphatically speech, speech purged of dross like gold in
the furnace, so it must have emphatically the essential elements of
speech' (LIV 220).

Though Hopkins's formulation of a poetics of speech sound probably
works best applied to his own verse, it also provides a well-rationalized
explanation of the conventional, historically fluid application of the
term 'poetry' not only to verse of the highest complexity like his, but also
to texts that have no formal verse features other than being divided
graphically into lines and/or stanzas, even texts in prose form. His
formulations of sprung rhythm indicate, further, how his own complex

forms with their careful timing relate to the most logaoedic and asymmetrical composition. In sum, his poetics provides a coherent and philosophically sophisticated explanation of the instinctive feeling of experienced poets, theorists, and readers that poetry reaches beyond the logical meanings of language. Beyond the world of the grammatical and logical lies one of feeling and of the human spirit, however that is defined. Like any searching explanation of worldly phenomena that rests on metaphysical arguments, his poetics of speech sound makes assumptions for which there are no empirical tests; at the same time, its originality and strength in providing answers to long-unanswered questions constitute significant evidence that in addition to being a major poet, Gerard Manley Hopkins is also a literary theorist of first importance.

Works Cited

Barnes, William. *An Outline of English Speechcraft*. London: Kegan, 1878.
– *The Poems of William Barnes*. 2 vols. Carbondale: Southern Illinois UP, 1962.
Beardsley, Monroe. *Aesthetics: Problems in the Philosophy of Criticism*. New York: Harcourt, 1958.
– 'Verse and Music.' *Versification: Major Language Types: Sixteen Essays*. Ed. William K. Wimsatt, Jr. New York: MLA, 1972. 238–50.
Bender, Todd K. *Gerard Manley Hopkins: The Classical Background and Critical Reception of His Work*. Baltimore: Johns Hopkins UP, 1966.
Bernstein, Leonard. *The Unanswered Questions: Six Talks at Harvard*. Cambridge: Harvard UP, 1976.
Bolinger, Dwight L. *Forms of English: Accent, Morpheme, Order*. Cambridge: Harvard UP, 1965.
– *Intonation and Its Parts*. Palo Alto: Stanford UP, 1986.
Brent, Joseph. *Charles Sanders Peirce: A Life*. Rev. ed. Bloomington: Indiana UP, 1998.
Bridges, Robert. *Milton's Prosody*. Rev. ed. Oxford: Oxford UP, 1921.
Brown, Daniel. *Hopkins' Idealism: Philosophy, Physics, Poetry*. Oxford: Clarendon, 1997.
Cable, Thomas. *The English Alliterative Tradition*. Philadelphia: U of Pennsylvania P, 1991.
Crocker, Richard. '*Musica Rhythmica* and *Musica Metrica* in Antique and Medieval Theory.' *Journal of Music Theory* 1 (1957): 2–23.
Culler, Jonathan. 'Presidential Forum.' *Professions 94*. New York: MLA, 1994. 3–12.
Dante Alighieri. *De Vulgari Eloquentia*. Ed. and trans. Robert S. Haller. *Literary Criticism of Dante Alighieri*. Lincoln: U of Nebraska P, 1973.
Deschamps, Eustache. *L'art de dictier*. In *Oeuvres complètes de Eustache Deschamps*. Vol. 7, 266–94. Ed. Gaston Raynaud. Société des anciens textes français. Paris: Firmin-Didot, 11 vols. 1878–1904.

Devlin, Christopher. 'The Image and the Word,' *Month* n.s. 3 (1950): 115–27+.

Dryden, John. 'An Essay of Dramatic Poesy.' *Critical Theory Since Plato*. Ed.
Hazard Adams. New York: Harcourt, 1971. 213–48.

Eliot, T.S. 'Hamlet and His Problems.' *Critiques and Essay in Criticism, 1920–48*.
Ed. Robert W. Stallman. New York: Ronald, 1949. 384–8.

– *The Music of Poetry*. The Third W.P. Ker Memorial Lecture. Glasgow: Jackson,
1942.

Ellsberg, Margaret. *Created to Praise: The Language of Gerard Manley Hopkins*. New
York: Oxford UP, 1987.

Erlich, Victor. *Russian Formalism: History and Doctrine*. 3rd ed. New Haven: Yale
UP, 1981.

Feeney, Joseph J., SJ. 'The Gerard Manley Hopkins Archive of the Harry Ransom Humanities Research Center.' *Hopkins Lives: An Exhibition and Catalogue*.
Ed. David Oliphant. Austin: Harry Ransom Humanities Research Center,
1989. 11–39.

Frost, Robert. *Robert Frost on Writing*. Ed. Elaine Barry. New Brunswick, NJ:
Rutgers UP, 1973.

Genette, Gérard. *Mimologies*. Trans. Thaïs E. Morgan. Lincoln: U of Nebraska P,
1995.

Grundlehner, Philip. *The Poetry of Friedrich Nietzsche*. London: Oxford UP,
1986.

Hagen, Lyman B. *Heart of a Woman, Mind of a Writer, and Soul of a Poet: A Critical
Analysis of the Writings of Maya Angelou*. Lanham, MD.: UP of America, 1997.

Hardison, O.B., Jr. *Prosody and Purpose in the English Renaissance*. Baltimore:
Johns Hopkins UP, 1989.

Hartman, Geoffrey H. 'Hopkins Revisited.' *Beyond Formalism: Literary Essays,
1958–1970*. Ed. Geoffrey H. Hartman. New Haven: Yale UP. 1970. 231–46.

– *The Unmediated Vision: An Interpretation of Wordsworth, Hopkins, Rilke and Valéry*.
New Haven: Yale UP, 1954.

Heaney, Seamus. 'The Drag of the Golden Chain.' *Times Literary Supplement*,
12 Nov., 1999, 14–16.

– *The Government of the Tongue*. London: Faber, 1988.

– *Preoccupations: Selected Prose, 1968–78*. London: Faber, 1980.

Hollahan, Eugene. *Hopkins against History*. Omaha, NE: Creighton UP, 1995.

Hollander, John. *In Time and Place*. Baltimore: Johns Hopkins UP, 1986.

Holloway, Sister Marcella Marie. *The Prosodic Theory of Gerard Manley Hopkins*.
Washington, DC: Catholic U of America P, 1947.

Hopkins, Gerard Manley. *The Correspondence of Gerard Manley Hopkins and Richard
Watson Dixon*. Ed. Claude Colleer Abbott. London: Oxford UP, 1935. [LII]

– *Further Letters of Gerard Manley Hopkins, Including His Correspondence with Coven-*

try Patmore. Ed. Claude Colleer Abbott. 2nd ed. London: Oxford UP, 1956.
[LIII]
– *Gerard Manley Hopkins: The Major Works*. Ed. Catherine Phillips. Oxford World
Classics. London: Oxford UP, 2002.
– *The Journals and Papers of Gerard Manley Hopkins*. Ed. Humphry House and
Graham Storey. London: Oxford UP, 1959. [J]
– *The Later Poetic Manuscripts of Gerard Manley Hopkins in Facsimile*. Ed. Norman
H. Mackenzie. New York: Garland P, 1991. [MSII]
– *The Letters of Gerard Manley Hopkins to Robert Bridges*. Ed. Claude Colleer Abbott.
London: Oxford UP, 1935. [LI]
– *The Poetical Works of Gerard Manley Hopkins*. Ed. Norman H. Mackenzie. Ox-
ford: Clarendon P, 1990. [P]
– *Selected Letters*. Ed. Catherine Phillips. Oxford: Clarendon P, 1990. [LIV]
Jakobson, Roman. 'A Few Remarks on Peirce, Pathfinder in the Science of
Language.' *Selected Writings*, Vol. 7. Ed. Stephen Rudy. Berlin: Mouton, 1985.
248–53.
– 'Linguistics and Poetics.' *Language in Literature*. Ed. Krystyna Pomorska and
Stephen Rudy. Cambridge: Belknap P, 1987. 18–51.
– 'Quest for the Essence of Language.' *Selected Writings*, Vol. 2. The Hague:
Mouton, 1970. 323–59.
– 'The Spell of Speech Sounds.' *Selected Writings*, Vol. 8. Ed. Stephen Rudy.
Berlin: Mouton, 1988. 181–239.
Jakobson, Roman, and Linda Waugh. *The Sound Shape of Language*. Brighton,
U.K.: Harvester P, 1976.
John of Garland. *The Parisiana Poetria*. Ed. and trans. Traugott Lawler. New
York: Yale UP, 1974.
Katz, Steven B. *The Epistemic Music of Rhetoric: Toward the Temporal Dimension of
Affect in Reader Response and Writing*. Carbondale: Southern Illinois UP, 1996.
Kiparsky, Paul. 'Sprung Rhythm.' *Phonetics and Phonology*. Vol. 1 of *Rhythm and
Meter*. Ed. Paul Kiparsky and Gilbert Youmans. San Diego: Academic P, 1988.
304–40.
Kristeva, Julia. *Desire in Language: A Semiotic Approach to Literature and Art*. Ed.
Leon S. Roudiez. Trans. Thomas Gora et al. New York: Columbia UP, 1980.
– *The Portable Kristeva*. Rev. ed. Ed. Kelly Oliver. New York: Columbia UP, 2002.
– *Revolution in Poetic Language*. Trans. Margaret Waller. Intro. by Leon S.
Roudiez. New York: Columbia UP, 1984.
Küper, Christoph. 'Linguistic Givens and Metrical Codes: Five Case Studies of
Their Linguistic and Aesthetic Relations.' *Poetics Today* (*Metrics Today* 2) 17
(1996): 89–126.
– *Walisische Traditionen in der Dichtung von G.M. Hopkins*. Bonn: Bouvier, 1973.

Langer, Suzanne. *Philosophy in a New Key: A Study in the Symbolism of Reason, Rite, and Art.* Cambridge, MA: Harvard UP, 1941.

Lichtmann, Maria R. *The Contemplative Poetry of Gerard Manley Hopkins.* Princeton: Princeton UP, 1989.

Lotman, Jurij. *The Structure of the Artistic Text.* Trans. Ronald Vroon. Michigan Slavic Contributions 7. Ann Arbor: U of Michigan Dept of Slav. Lang. and Lit. 1977.

Lowes, John Livingston. *Convention and Revolt in Poetry.* London: Houghton, 1938.

MacKenzie, Norman H. 'Hopkins and St. Dorothea: Lines for Whose Picture?' *Vital Candle: Victorian and Modern Bearings on Gerard Manley Hopkins.* Waterloo, ON: U of Waterloo P, 1984. 32–9.

Mackey, Louis. *Peregrinations of the Word: Essays in Medieval Philosophy.* Ann Arbor: U of Michigan P, 1997.

Mayakovsky, Vladimir. *How Are Verses Made?* Trans. G.M. Hyde. London: Cape, 1970.

Miller, J. Hillis. *The Linguistic Moment: from Wordsworth to Stevens.* Princeton: Princeton UP, 1985.

– 'The Universal Chiming.' *Hopkins: A Collection of Critical Essays.* Ed. Geoffrey H. Hartman. Englewood Cliffs, NJ: Prentice-Hall, 1966. 89–116.

Milroy, James. *The Language of Gerard Manley Hopkins.* London: Deutsch, 1977.

Milton, John. *Complete Poems and Major Prose.* Ed. Merritt Y. Hughes. New York: Odyssey, 1957.

Milward, Peter, S.J. *Landscape and Inscape: Vision and Inspiration in Hopkins's Poetry.* London: Elek, 1975.

Müller, Max. *Lectures on the Science of Language.* 1st ser. London: Longman, 1861. 2nd ser., 1863.

New Princeton Encyclopedia of Poetry and Poetics. Ed. Alex Preminger, T.V.F. Brogan, et al. Princeton: Princeton UP, 1993.

Nietzsche, Friedrich. *The Birth of Tragedy, and The Case of Wagner.* Trans. Walter Kaufmann. New York: Vintage, 1967.

– *The Gay Science.* Trans. Walter Kaufmann. New York: Vintage, 1974.

O'Donoghue, Bernard. *Seamus Heaney and the Language of Poetry.* New York: Harcourt, 1994.

Ong, Walter J., SJ. 'Hopkins' Sprung Rhythm and the Life of English Poetry.' *Immortal Diamond: Studies in Gerard Manley Hopkins.* Ed. Norman Weyand, SJ. London: Sheed, 1949. 93–174.

Parker, John Henry. *A Concise Glossary of Terms Used in Grecian, Roman and Gothic Architecture.* 2nd ed. Oxford: Oxford UP, 1866.

Pater, Walter. 'The School of Giorgione.' *Fortnightly Review.* New ser. 1 (1877): 2.

Patmore, Coventry. *Coventry Patmore's 'Essay on English Metrical Laws'*. Ed. Sister Mary Augustine Roth. Washington, DC: Catholic UP, 1961.

Peirce, Charles Sanders. *Collected Papers of Charles Sanders Peirce.* Ed. Charles Hartshorne, Paul Weiss, and A. Burke. 8 vols. Cambridge: Harvard UP. 1931–58.

– *The Essential Peirce: Selected Philosophical Writings.* Vol. 1 (1867–93). Ed. Nathan Houser and Christian Kloesel. Bloomington: Indiana UP, 1992.

– *Philosophical Writings of Peirce.* Ed. Justus Buchler. New York: Dover, 1955.

– *Writings of C.S. Peirce.* Ed. Max Fisch et al. 5 vols to date. Bloomington: Indiana UP, 1982–

Plato. *The Timaeus of Plato.* Ed. R.-D. Archer-Hind. Rpt. N.Y.: Arno, 1972 [1888].

Plotkin, Cary H. *The Tenth Muse: Victorian Philology and the Genesis of the Poetic Language of Gerard Manley Hopkins.* Carbondale: Southern Illinois UP, 1989.

Roberts, Gerald. *Gerard Manley Hopkins: A Literary Life.* Houndmills, UK: Macmillan, 1994.

Sapir, Edward. 'The Musical Foundations of Verse.' *Journal of English and Germanic Philology* 20 (1921): 213–18.

Saussure, Ferdinand de. *Cours de linguistique générale.* Ed. Charles Bally and Albert Sechehaye, with Albert Riedlinger. Critical Edition, Tullio Mauro. 4th ed. Paris: Payot, 1949.

Schneider, Elizabeth. *The Dragon in the Gate.* Berkeley: U of California P, 1968.

Sheriff, John K. *The Fate of Meaning: Charles Peirce, Structuralism, and Literature.* Princeton: Princeton UP, 1989.

Sprinker, Michael. *A Counterpoint of Dissonance: The Aesthetics and Poetry of Gerard Manley Hopkins.* Baltimore: Johns Hopkins UP, 1980.

Steiner, George. *After Babel: Aspects of Language and Translation.* 2nd ed. Oxford: Oxford UP, 1992.

– *Grammars of Creation.* London: Faber, 2001.

Stevens, John. 'Gerard Manley Hopkins as Musician.' Hopkins, *The Journals and Papers of Gerard Manley Hopkins* [J]. 457–97.

Stevens, Wallace. *Opus Posthumous.* Rev. ed. Ed. Milton Bates. New York: Knopf, 1989.

Valéry, Paul. *Art of Poetry.* Trans. Denise Foliot. New York: Pantheon, 1958.

– *Leonardo, Poe, Mallarmé.* Trans. Malcolm Cowley and James R. Lawler. Princeton: Princeton UP, 1972.

Vivas, Eliseo. 'The Objective Correlative of T.S. Eliot.' *Critiques and Essays in Criticism, 1920–48.* Ed. R.W. Stallman. New York: Ronald P, 1949. 389–400.

Weaver, Bennett. 'Shelley Works Out the Rhythm of "A Lament."' *PMLA* 47 (1932): 570–6.

Weinsheimer, Joel. 'A Word Is Not a Sign: Hermeneutics, Semiotics, and

Peirce's Ethics of Terminology.' *Peirce's Doctrine of Signs: Theory, Applications, and Connections.* Ed. Vincent Colapietro and Thomas M. Olshevsky. Approaches to Semiotics 123. Berlin: Mouton, 1991. 399–413.

White, Norman. *Hopkins: A Literary Biography.* Oxford: Clarendon, 1992.

Wimsatt, James I. 'Alliteration and Hopkins's Sprung Rhythm.' *Poetics Today* 19 (1998): 531–64.

– 'John Duns Scotus, Charles Sanders Peirce, and Chaucer's Portraits of the Canterbury Pilgrims.' *Speculum* 71 (1996): 633–46. [1996a]

– 'Rhyme, the Icons of Sound, and the Middle English *Pearl.*' *Style* 30 (1996): 189–219. [1996b]

– 'Rhyme/Reason, Chaucer/Pope, Icon/Symbol,' *Modern Language Quarterly* 55 (1994): 17–46.

Wimsatt, William K., Jr. 'The Rule and the Norm: Halle and Keyser on Chaucer's Meter.' *Literary Style: A Symposium.* Ed. Seymour Chatman. London: Oxford UP, 1971. 197–215.

– *The Verbal Icon: Studies in the Meaning of Poetry.* Lexington: U of Kentucky P, 1954.

Index